Odyssey of a Law School

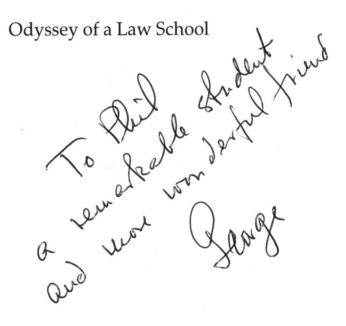

To Phil
a remarkable student
and more wonderful friend
George

ODYSSEY OF A LAW SCHOOL

A Personal History of
California Western School of Law,
its Exotic Voyage Past Theosophy,
African Gold and an Elks Hall

George N. Gafford
Professor Emeritus

Published by
Mountain N' Air Books
La Crescenta, CA 91214

Published by
  Mountain N' Air Books
  P.O. Box 12540
  La Crescenta, CA 91224
  (800) 446-9696 – Fax: (800) 303-5578
  E-mail: books@mountain-n-air.com

Cover Art: Stained glass California Western School of Law window, 1975. Designed by Mark Dennis and executed by Leslie Barrett, in memory of author's daughter Diane. 45" x 48"

Cover design by Gilberto d'Urso.

Book layout and design by Naomi Blackburn.

10 9 8 7 6 5 4 3 2 1

Library of Congress Control Number: 2001095017

ISBN: 1-879415-34-8

Acknowledgments

First of all I wish to acknowledge and thank William Sullivan for his great help and incentive in research of the early history of Balboa University. Also, Richard Lareau and Robert Dunn provided me with many recollections of their relationships with the university after it became California Western and with William Rust, its president.

Many members of the faculty and staff of the law school have been most helpful, William Price and Naomi Meir reproduced photographs old and new with great skill and care, and the Internet and *Timetables of History* reminded me of many of the noteworthy events on the world's stage during the odyssey of the law school.

But most of all I must acknowledge with thanks the encouragement, patience and advice of my loving wife, Martha.

Preface

This is the story of a school of most humble beginnings. It is not about one of the great and venerable institutions whose alumni predictably become the political leaders and industrial titans of the nation. But it is the story of a little proprietary night school which became a local university, then an international one, and then was bought away from that university to become a free-standing institution, a truly unique and outstanding law school. It is an entity whose life has not even been as long as mine, but may be of more universal interest than the revered halls of learning about which so much is written.

A law school is a living institution, changing students with changing goals and obsessions. It is a microcosm of society itself, and the metamorphosis of what began as a tiny night law school reveals many of the permutations of American life in the past seventy-five years.

This then is not simply a history, but the story of a most unusual and exotic voyage. It combines some of the philosophical thoughts nurtured through a most varied life with the vicissitudes of the school in its odyssey through the greater part of the last century of the millennium.

Table of Contents

Chapter I

Balboa Law School Is Born

Early in 1924, in the then sleepy Navy town near the Mexican border called San Diego (population less than 150,000), Dr. Margaret Whitworth established and incorporated the very short-lived San Diego Chiropractic College. In those days of few government regulations, the corporation had degree-granting rights, rights which were later to become important, after the chiropractic college was no longer operational.

Woodrow Wilson and Joseph Conrad died in 1924, Hitler was sentenced to five years' imprisonment, Ford sold his ten millionth car, J. Edgar Hoover was appointed director of the Bureau of Investigation (later renamed the Federal Bureau of Investigation), George Gershwin finished *Lady Be Good* and Sigmund Romberg's *Student Prince* was on Broadway.

Among the many artists actively painting, writing and composing in that year were Georges Braque, Marc Chagall, the Maurices Utrillo, Vlaminck and Ravel, Igor Stravinsky, E.M. Forster, Joan Miro, Paul Klee, Pablo Picasso, Franz Lehar, Bela Bartok, Noel Coward, Raoul Dufy, John Marin, Edward Hopper, George Grosz, Jan Sibelius, Edvard Munch and Henri Matisse.

Three years later, Fred D. Finn, the principal of San Diego High School, was driving, and Leland Ghent Stanford, a fledgling 26-year-old attorney at the firm of Luce and Swing on Broadway, was his passenger. As the two headed south from Los Angeles, they watched the twilight turn to darkness and talked of the teaching enterprise they would bring into being in the fall.

The road from Los Angeles to San Diego was narrow and tortuous, a single lane in each direction, and with a hill at Torrey Pines which few automobiles could manage without shifting down to a lower gear.

Earlier that day, the State of California department of education's Los Angeles office had granted Stanford accreditation to teach the new Bar preparatory class at San Diego Evening High. In the era before the junior college system, San Diego Evening High offered job-oriented courses to adults working or hoping to work in trades, businesses and professions. Classes were held at the San Diego High School building, reverently called the Gray Castle.

San Diego needed a school to give good quality law courses, not just for those who wanted to be lawyers but for all kinds of young people in the business and professional worlds. There was then no law school in California south of Los Angeles. Stanford, a truly brilliant individual, undoubtedly saw opportunities for himself financially and professionally in establishing such a school.

The concept of a Balboa University in Balboa Park had been put forth some time before. For better or for worse, it did not work out because of the problem of security, at least that is what Stanford said in his 1968 book, *San Diego's Legal Lore and the Bar*. Florence Christman, in her charming book *Balboa Park: Its Romance and Whatever* said a move to locate San Diego College in the park was "squelched."

The idea for a law preparatory class at San Diego Evening High had come from some one hundred or so students in a business law course offered there in the 1926-27 school year. While classes would be offered under the supervision of the San Diego public schools which would pay the meager salaries of the instructors, the classes would have the identity, however unofficial, of Balboa Law College. A stand-up sign in the hallway outside the classrooms would proclaim that fact.

Ten consecutive law courses were given each year, and the fee for the mimeographed syllabus for each course was $7. Attorney Bertrand L. Comparet began a 21-year stint as an instructor with the start of the 1928-29 school year, and Frank Buckley was added to the faculty in the 1929-30 term. One of Balboa's first adult students was Ida I. Dolph, a partner with Jean B. Cooper in the Book Nook, an early bookstore at 1239 Fifth Avenue. Dolph was apparently interested in learning something about law as an adjunct to her business. Cooper's aunt Freddie (more formally Frederika A. Cooper) was one of San Diego's first women jurors.

In 1930, a construction worker named DeWitt A. Higgs (born in Idaho in 1907) moved to San Diego with the woman he had married in the Nevada desert town of Winnemucca. Higgs drove a dynamite truck by day to put himself through the Balboa Law School at night. He later founded one of San Diego's finest law firms. Higgs was a Regent of the University of California and one of the early trustees of California Western School of Law—part of and later purchased from United States International University, formerly known as California Western University, the direct descendent of Balboa Law School!

Leland Stanford brought in, at his own expense, local judges and lawyers and occasional out-of-town authorities to lecture at the school. On January 23, 1930, a local newspaper reported Balboa's annual banquet, held that evening at the San Diego Athletic Club. The club building later became the executive offices of United States International University (where I was interviewed thirty-nine years later by Dr. William Rust, its president, before joining the university's law school faculty). Many years after that, with the university in financial trouble, the building was sold and painted light blue and white, to become the headquarters of Harcourt, Brace, Jovanovich Inc.

It was also reported that at Balboa's 1930 banquet Judge Eugene Daney, Sr., of the Board of Governors of the California State Bar, was to speak on "Legal Ethics". In addition, six Superior Court judges would respond to toasts, among them:

Judge C. N. Andrews: "The Lawyer in Court"

Judge Lacey D. Jennings: "The Lawyer in Business"
Judge Lloyd Griffin: "The Lawyer at Play"[1]
Judge A.C. Finney: "The Lawyer in Politics"

The toastmaster for the evening was Paul V. Tuttle. Like many students at Balboa, Tuttle had been a practicing attorney elsewhere, in his case on the Atlantic Coast, and had enrolled to prepare for the California Bar exam. The newspaper report of the evening described Balboa as "San Diego's only institution offering complete preparation for the California Bar examinations" and that it was "under the jurisdiction of the state public school system."

It was further reported at about that time that after the classes had been organized by Leland G. Stanford in 1927, the response of the public was so wholehearted that several hundred students were registered after classes were first opened. Stanford later stated that the enrollment in 1930 was 140 law students.

Beginning in September, 1927, the advanced class studied three nights each week. New classes were added from time to time, which made it necessary to add new instructors, which ultimately gave the institution, as a newspaper reported: "a real collegiate significance."

Balboa's good days were short, however, for it came on hard times with the onset of the Depression. Major university law schools suffered drops in enrollment and consequent drops in tuition revenues. Unaffiliated and proprietary law schools like Balboa were seen as competition. In the case of Balboa, pressure was brought to bear in the form of letters to school authorities.

As a result, Stanford was told that the school system could no longer continue to back Balboa Law School. He refused to accept that verdict without a fight. After much cajoling, he successfully won an agreement from the school system to rent classroom space for $1 per night. In the meantime he looked about for a means to develop an institution capable of granting law degrees on its own.

---

[1] Many years later, the Eastern Star of the Masons gave an annual scholarship at California Western School of Law in Judge Griffin's name to a deserving student with a Masonic background.

Money, as the Depression continued, proved to be the greatest stumbling block in the path of expansion, for incorporation would cost many unavailable depression dollars. By great good fortune, a state official in Sacramento friendly to Stanford offered a possible solution:

"There's a chiropractic college in San Diego which is about to lose its charter for non-payment of state franchise taxes. It has the right to grant degrees. Maybe you could buy it without the expense of incorporation."

The first directors of that corporation were the attorney and four chiropractors. It had been incorporated by a local counselor, Judge Durelle Fernando Glidden, and it was through him that Dr. Margaret Whitworth, the sole owner, transferred the charter to Stanford. Glidden had had his B.A. and M.A. degrees before he became a lawyer, and had been the co-organizer of the Michigan State Bar Association. He had served in Michigan as commissioner and judge before he became prominent in San Diego as prosecutor of the notorious I.W.W. cases. Glidden never had any connection with Balboa Law School.

Stanford negotiated the deal with Dr. Whitworth. For $100 the degree-granting rights of San Diego Chiropractic College were obtained by the purchase of the non-operational corporation and its charter. It was that charter, drafted by Judge Glidden (amended and broadened in 1933), which was the authorization of every degree granted by Balboa and California Western University, later named United States International University!

Austere for a while, through Stanford's efforts the school's prospects began again to improve. In the spring of 1934, the trustees announced the formation of a scholarship fund. In September, the San Diego Union reported that George Al Berry and Jerome Niederman, both students at San Diego State, had been selected as scholarship recipients. The 1933-1934 enrollment was then said to be 65 students.

The last Balboa Law School classes at San Diego High were held in 1935. In the fall of that year, the school leased space from Kelsey-Jenny, a business school then operating on C Street in San Diego, between 10th and 11th Avenues, next to the later YWCA building.

An advertisement in the newspaper in September, 1936, announced the start of the fall term for Balboa Law College, with the first meeting to be held in Russ Auditorium. The ad further proclaimed: "This institution is the only law college in San Diego. It begins its eleventh year this fall and has the honor of having the highest official rating of all evening law schools in California in the success of its students in the state bar examinations."

In 1937, the school was accredited by the state with the passing of Chapter 503 of the statutes of that year. The Committee of Bar Examiners included Balboa Law College among the twelve accredited schools in California. The accreditation was based on three criteria: the percentage of successful Balboa applicants taking the bar the first time, the authority of Balboa to grant professional degrees, and Balboa's offering of a curriculum requiring classroom attendance!

Among the non-accredited were the correspondence schools, "campuses without walls."

As a result of that accreditation, Balboa's students were exempt from the preliminary examination after their first year which was then required of students in non-accredited schools.

Despite his valiant efforts on behalf of the school and its success, Leland Stanford's career as president came to grief in the spring of 1939, when the San Diego County grand jury investigated his handling of the estate of the late Edwin Stevens for his widow, Jennie Stevens.

"This all comes from my attempt to help out a woman and do a kindness," Stanford told the newspaper. "Any charge they have against me is a purely technical one." District Attorney James B. Abbey leveled charges that Stanford had taken a total of $11,481 from the Stevens estate between July, 1936, and May, 1939, which he used for the purchase of a home and later upkeep and repairs. He was found guilty of some of the charges by Judge Charles C. Haines (who had been a speaker at the 1930 Balboa banquet!).

Judge Haines said he "...believed Stanford had no intention of carrying out his promise of making a mortgage to secure Mrs. Stevens for $10,000 borrowed to purchase Stanford's West Palm Street home..." and that his conduct constituted fraud.

The judge must not have felt quite as strongly as he sounded, however, for he gave Stanford probation and a two-year suspended sentence, and it was reported in the San Diego Union that "Judge Charles C. Haines...said that the prosecution's case was a technical one...that he had not liked Stanford's attitude toward the Stevens matter and his apparent feeling that he was totally without blame."

The judge continued: "I doubt that his impulses were bad. He apparently let self-interest get the better of his judgment when dealing with a client, something all lawyers have to guard against."

Judge Haines then pointed out that the legal profession must be rigid in upholding its honor. That was over sixty years ago, and the same problem certainly still exists today—except that today the general public has much less confidence in attorneys than it did then.

Rightly or wrongly in that particular case, Judge Haines appears to have demanded the highest punctilio of honor in the profession. Perhaps if the courts and the bar itself, throughout the last sixty years, had been as strict and unforgiving as Judge Haines, there would be a more profound adherence to the absolute integrity and professionalism which their fiduciary position of trust requires of lawyers. Unless there is a total observance of those standards, without exception or equivocation, the true value of attorneys to society and society's attitudes toward them will not improve.

"I for one," Judge Haines said in an interview, "have not lost confidence in Mr. Stanford. I am hopeful he may practice again."

Unfortunately, such was not to be the case. He had ceased to practice law in the spring of 1939, organized and operated a law publishing company for some ten years, after which he became San Diego County Law Librarian.

He was held in exceptionally high regard by the San Diego Bar, and served the library with distinction until he retired in 1971.

Chapter II

Dwight Stanford Takes Over

After Leland Stanford left Balboa Law School, his brother Dwight became Dean and ran the school out of his law offices in the Hillcrest area of San Diego.

When Dwight Stanford took over the reins of Balboa Law School in 1939, he was stung by the criticism that the school was a "proprietary" institution, owned and operated for the benefit and profit of the Stanford family.[2]

Running a law school, Stanford learned, was a tough, competitive, dog-eat-dog business. Schools, their representatives and alumni could and would try to make things tough for other schools, either through official channels or unofficially in off-the-record, behind-the-scenes conversations among graduates, alumni or prospective students. (The extents to which that competitiveness can go were certainly demonstrated and will be seen later in the odyssey of the law school when we come to the time there were efforts to merge California Western into the University of California.)

---

[2] In Cleveland, Ohio, there were two proprietary night law schools. Judge Willis Vickery was the principal founder, in 1897, of the Baldwin University Law School (called the Cleveland Law School after 1899), followed as dean by his son, Melville, and then by Judge Lee E. Skeel. Judge David C. Meck, Sr., founded John Marshall School of Law in 1916, with five students, and was succeeded as dean by his son, Judge David C. Meck, Jr. Having been operated as competing family businesses, but now stung by the same sort of criticism, and being more interested in building a fine law school than profiting themselves, the owners in 1946 merged the two schools to become Cleveland-Marshall Law School, (at which I taught for many years). It was then unhappily merged with Baldwin-Wallace University for a short time, then disaffiliated, and some years later, as Cleveland-Marshall College of Law, became a part of Cleveland State University, where it is a fully accredited front-line law school.

The youngest of the three attorney sons of dairyman Ira E. Stanford, Dwight was thirteen years younger then Leland and twenty years younger then his brother Joy. He had been a Tau Sigma, and president of Phi Lambda at San Diego State. In 1936, he had received degrees from both San Diego State and Balboa Law School, and was admitted to the California Bar before departing for Stanford University in the fall to study for his Master of Arts degree in political science.

In March of 1937, he took time off from his studies to marry the former Maxine Harris in a large wedding at Central Christian Church with seven attendants on either side of the altar. The couple honeymooned at Idyllwild and Del Monte before heading back to Stanford University.

Dwight Sanford was twenty-five years old when he inherited Balboa Law School and its problems in 1939.

One of his first goals was to raise the school out of the proprietary class and make it into a university for all of San Diego. When he took over from his brother Leland there were but four students who attended school in his offices in the bank building at 3911 Fifth Avenue. He persuaded five more students to join him, for a student body of nine, among whom were John Martin, Roy Cleator and Joe McDonough. McDonough later became a member of the California Bar and an instructor at the school.

Elizabeth C. MacPhail, then legal secretary to the Mayor of San Diego, enrolled at Balboa the following year. This is what she said in an interview given to the San Diego Historical Society in 1975:

"So I decided I would go to law school. I probably had regretted that I had not gone on to college, and yet I didn't want to go to the only college that was here (San Diego State), and I could not afford to go away.

"The only law school here at that time was Balboa Law School. It was in a bank building at Fifth and University and was run by the Stanfords, Dwight, Leland and Joy, and it was a four-year night school.

"I started in law school in the fall of 1940, and during those four years, it was during the height of the War, and I can remember having to go to night school some nights when we had blackouts and we had to drive without any lights, and that was really nervewracking. Fortunately, I didn't live too far away.

"The classes were held for three nights a week."

MacPhail, who lived with her parents on Panorama Drive, rode to class with Cecil Holley, a 1944 graduate who worked as a police officer. Another classmate was Richard B. Ault, then a school teacher with two children. Dwight Stanford suggested to Ault that he study law. He had done his undergraduate work at San Diego State, graduating in 1938, and going on to the University of California where he received his M.A. in 1940. Moving to the part-time study of the law at night, he received his LL. B. from Balboa in 1946.[3]

Other students at Balboa at the time included Ray Waunsley, who became a CPA and a City Council member, and Verne O. "Pop" Warner, who received special permission to take the bar examination after three years of school. His wife was pregnant with their first child, a boy, who would later become a lawyer in San Francisco. "Pop" Warner became a Superior Court judge.

Attorney John Cranston, later a senior member of San Diego's then largest law firm, Gray, Carey, Ames and Fry and a member of the Board of Trustees of United States International University, Balboa's progeny, was Ault's contracts professor. Other prominent practicing attorneys like Jim Toothaker (who became a Superior Court judge) taught torts, and Ed Stropp taught wills.

Following the formal class sessions, Ault recalled, the students would retire to the beer bar across the street, or else go around the corner to the bowling alley, where they would discuss the current class subjects until late into the night.

---

[3] Ault later became a distinguished justice of the California Court of Appeal and, some thirty years after graduating from Balboa, the first Chairman of the Board of California Western School of Law after its purchase from United States International University.

From that law school, with the judges and practicing lawyers who were its teachers, and the students from all walks of life, many from humbler parts of the ordinary world, came men and women aspiring to make a new life for themselves and their families. Whether or not they knew it, they were to become the spokespersons for their generation.

Chapter III

Balboa Law School Becomes a University

In Southern California, on the far away West Coast which I had not then ever even hoped to see, Balboa University continued to operate up to and through World War II. The airplane industry grew and prospered in San Diego, thousands of men and women moved into the area from all over the country, but especially from Oklahoma and Texas—so many that it was said that if someone in the Convair bomber plant called out, "Hey, Tex" a half-dozen Texans would drop an airplane part on an Okie's foot.

The sleepy little Navy town began to hum with activity in the war plants and the Navy and Marine bases, as well as in the shipyards. As more and more men were drafted, women began taking their places, and Rosie the Riveter was born. With the influx of workers, as the servicemen's dependents began moving in, housing became tight, restaurants and bars became crowded, San Diego began bursting at its seams.

And after the Japanese bombed Pearl Harbor on December 7, 1941, when the war actually came to our country, it seemed as if almost everyone in the Navy or Marine Corps trained in, was stationed in or passed through San Diego. When it was reported that a Japanese submarine had lobbed a shell over Santa Barbara, the fear of attack became a plausible reality, and black-out conditions were imposed. All cars drove with dim, shielded lights at night, and all windows had to be covered so that light could not escape. Most dramatic of all, Pacific Highway and the waterfront were completely camouflaged by enormous sheets of netting suspended on posts over the entire dock and bay area. The netting was so painted as to change the entire outline of the coast—making the exact location of the long expanse of the Convair plants, the shipyards and the warship bases impossible to determine from the air.

The treachery of Japan and the terrible fear of spies and sabotage on the West Coast were so great that as wrong as it now seems to have been, the U.S. government moved more than 100,000 Niseis (second-generation Japanese) to inland camps. On the East Coast the FBI captured eight German saboteurs who had landed in Florida and New York.

War having been declared against Japan, Germany and Italy, U.S. Savings Bonds and Stamps went on sale, and after the Office of Price Administration (OPA) had been established to regulate prices, the price of steel was frozen and rubber rationing was instituted. The entire mood of the country was changing as we comprehended the realities of our engagement in a global all-out war. The movie *Mrs. Miniver* made the British escape of 340,000 men from Dunkirque real for Americans, and then we saw the soul-wrenching suffering and ignominy of the Bataan Death March forced on American and Philippine prisoners by the Japanese.

Unknown to most of us, the "Manhattan Project" of intense atomic research had begun, Enrico Fermi had split the atom, the first electronic brain or automatic computer was developed, and magnetic recording tape was invented. The U.S. Supreme Court upheld the Federal Wage and Hour Law restricting the work of 16 and 18-year-olds and setting minimum wages for businesses engaged in interstate commerce.

In 1941 and 1942, the popular songs were *Bewitched, Bothered and Bewildered, Deep in the Heart of Texas, I Don't Want to Set the World on Fire, Chattanooga Choo-Choo, White Christmas, I Left My Heart at the Stage Door Canteen, White Cliffs of Dover, Praise the Lord and Pass the Ammunition, Paper Doll,* and *That Old Black Magic.*

Dwight Stanford, Balboa University's president, stated that in the midst of the early turmoil of the War, Albert Fibiger should be credited with the impetus that led to the founding of the School of Accounting of Balboa sometime in 1942. Fibiger had been in public accounting since 1918, and had had his own Certified Public Accounting firm since 1929.

According to Stanford, Fibiger said San Diego lacked a school where an accountant could study for the CPA examination. If Stanford and the Balboa trustees (which included Fibiger) would set up a CPA program under the Balboa banner, Fibiger promised to staff it with two or three of the best certified public accountants in the city.

The idea appealed to Stanford and the board, and the School of Accounting was started. The courses offered included accounting, theory, taxes, and auditing. Enrollment was given a major boost when Byron M. Miller, was hired from Convair. By 1944, it was recognized that even with a law school and a school of accounting, Balboa could not logically be called a university without a liberal arts program. But more time had to pass before such a program could become a reality.

With the end of World War II in 1945, came a dramatic increase in enrollment as the G.I. Bill of Rights gave the promise of a college education, and even graduate school, to service men and women returning to civilian life. Among those was Frank Orfield, who taught typing while he studied law, and later became business manager of Balboa.[4]

Busy Balboa University found itself doing business in an assortment of five buildings scattered around the crowded Hillcrest area of San Diego. Two were the property of the university, while the other three were rented. With the tuition at $35 per quarter, the G.I. Bill proved to be a mixed blessing. It brought more students and more prosperity, but it also brought a cash flow problem because the government's check for G.I student tuition was only sent quarterly, usually four or five weeks after the quarter ended.

President Stanford found a remedy to the situation with banker Spencer Smith, who provided short-term loans when needed to keep the school afloat. As Balboa grew, the need for a larger campus became

---

[4] Frank Orfield later became a judge of the Superior Court and Chairman of the Board of California Western School of Law after its purchase from USIU.

evident. Options were studied from nearby Reynard Way to an about-to-be-abandoned Army base in Campo. Campo was too far away.

The spring of 1947 saw the formation of Balboa's first athletic team, the Explorers, a softball group that got into the City Recreation Department League. This was also the year that George Wood died. Wood was a Coronado building contractor among whose assets was the former property of the Theosophical Institute on Point Loma.

By 1948, Balboa University began really to feel the pinch of students versus limited space. The library was located on Fourth Avenue, offices and two or three classrooms were located in barn-like rooms in the 3900 block of Fifth Avenue. A quonset hut erected by Dwight Stanford was divided into two more classrooms. Stanford himself and the law school faculty occupied office space in the Security Pacific Bank Building at the corner of University and Fifth Avenues.

That arrangement was improved upon with the acquisition of the Red Cross Building some blocks away in the 3600 block of Fifth Avenue. Its two modern classrooms featured then-contemporary lighting, new desks, large blackboards, and other conveniences. The so-called sunken garden outside became a haven for study and bull sessions.

After the barren rooms in the 3900 block of Fifth Avenue were razed, several neat little office buildings and a single classroom were erected in their stead The famous quonset hut was remodeled with plywood partitions creating three classrooms which were smaller but trimmer and warmer than what had been there before.

In the January 11, 1949 edition of the *Explorers' Log*, the Balboa student newspaper, the editor reported that he had been told by President Stanford that the private, non-profit educational institution had made a profit in 1948! The "profit" was used for purchasing books for Balboa's library, for erecting new classrooms, and for obtaining property for the school.

While the School of Business (now including the accounting school) flourished in that business-conscious era, the School of Law barely treaded water. In that same year, 1948, a democratic student government was formed for the first time, with Student Council officers from every class from both the schools of business and law. The School of Business was expanded to a four-year school offering a Bachelor's degree, and a Department of Liberal Arts was finally added, later called the College of Letters, Arts and Sciences, with a program leading to a Bachelor of Arts degree.

In March, 1949, a check of enrollments showed Balboa with a student body of 611, including 353 in the School of Business and 258 in the School of Law. There were both day and night school divisions, and the enrollments were almost equal, with 312 day students and 299 night.

While the School of Law had more graduates in the Class of 1949 than the School of Business, thirty-two to twenty-three in both day and night combined, it was becoming clear that students wanted Balboa to be a true university, much more than a law school. The fifteen day law school graduates had been a class of sixty when they matriculated in the fall of 1947. Illness, the need to work and poor grades had taken their toll.

In August of 1933, the Articles of Incorporation of the corporation originally named San Diego Chiropractic College in 1924, had been amended to change the corporate name to Balboa Graduate University, and in 1950 amended again to change the name to Balboa University.

Vernal Humphreys and Hal Kennedy led the formation of the Balboa Speakers' Club by the Class of 1949. Other members as of the spring of 1949 were John M. Riley, William E. Ferguson and William Yale.[5]

Ferguson, Humphreys, Wayne V. Hoy, Riley and Victor E. Urias constituted the membership of Omega Beta Beta, the honorary legal fraternity aimed at promoting scholarship and strong ties between students and alumni.

---

[5] William Yale also became a Superior Court judge, was an early trustee of California Western School of Law after its purchase from USIU, and a prominent arbitrator.

Three-person slates of class officers serving over the life of the Class of '49 included Riley, Dick Adams, Robert Miller, Hoy, Urias, Yale, Sunshine Summers, Ferguson and Robert Mason.

The faculty of the School of Law in the spring of 1949 included the following twelve individuals: Charles D. Holliday, LL.B., Dean and Professor; Dwight E Stanford, M.A., LL.B., Professor; Richard F Boyer, LL.B., Assistant Professor; Bertran L. Comparet, J.D., Assistant Professor; Homer Herz. LL. B., Assistant Professor; Richard B. Ault, M.A., LL.B., Instructor; Robert L. Barbour, LL.B., Instructor; Jack A. Brant, LL.B., Instructor; Robert W. Conyers, LL.B., Instructor[6]; Philip Crittenden, LL.B., C.P.A., Instructor; Edwin C. Jeffries, LL.B., Instructor; and Joseph P. McDonough, LL.B., Instructor.

All were members of the California Bar except Boyer, who was a member of the Iowa Bar. Dean Holliday taught equity and real property in the day school, and was tentatively scheduled to teach a bar review course in the summer of 1949 with Comparet and Herz.

Boyer taught corporations in the day school and Comparet taught torts in the night school and conflict of laws in the day school. Herz taught constitutional law in the night school and torts and evidence in the day school. Jeffries taught securities in the day school and McDonough taught sales in the night school.

As the fall quarter got under way in 1949, the new School of Liberal Arts offered courses in English, political science, mathematics, history, psychology and sociology. The School of Law, which had been the forefather of the entire school, was beginning to look smaller than its university brethren as several new members were added to the Liberal Arts faculty—but only two to the law faculty: John Flick and Richard Mackay.

Next came important shifts in the law school. Homer Herz was appointed executive assistant to the law school dean, the program was changed to three years, with classes to run nine months each year, and a ceiling on total enrollment of 150 students was imposed. Two

---

6 Robert Conyers was another distinguished San Diego judge with Balboa connections

years of college were required for admission, with a preference for the following subjects: accounting, economics, English composition, contemporary American literature, science, American history and government, sociology, corporate finance, and public speaking.

As the first classes of the new session (the 26th fall in Balboa's history) were being called to order, the news broke that Balboa University intended to buy the 195-acre grounds of the International Theosophical Institute's former headquarters on Point Loma for the new home of the university.

Kenneth S. Ray, an instructor in economics, acting as Research Director and Assistant to the President, had journeyed to San Francisco to work out a purchase agreement with the widow and daughter of the late George W. Wood.

The easy part was getting Sarah A. Wood and Rose V. Vollmer to agree to a purchase price which the university could afford. The 195-acre cliff-top ocean-view tract would be sold for $200,000, with a $50,000 down payment. Clare Banta and Judge Clarence Harden of the Board of Trustees were persuaded to come forward with the necessary cash, after a fund-raising drive was launched under marketing Assistant Professor Douglas Cook.

The hardest part of the sale had to do with talking the city of San Diego into allowing the property to be re-zoned to permit construction of multiple-unit buildings. The area was restricted to one-family dwellings. Ray took the Balboa proposal to City Hall, where the Planning Department listened to his presentation, but made no decision.

Dwight Stanford and the trustees met with a group of Point Loma property owners and argued that Balboa would be a good neighbor to all Point Loma residents. As it was, the then owners of the property in question were unable to keep the trees and shrubs in good condition and Stanford pointed out that the once-beautiful grounds had become overgrown and an eyesore.

The owners needed to sell the property, and they could either sell to an institution such as the university, or they could break up the beautiful expanse of real estate into individual lots and destroy it forever. The wisdom of bringing Balboa into Point Loma was clear to many property owners, but there were reservations about the re-zoning proposal. Committees were appointed from both sides. The talks went on.

So did the worry. A mortgage of $150,000 or more (for it began to look as though it would be difficult to come up with the originally agreed-upon $50,000 down payment) would put Balboa into a financial position unprecedented in the history of the conservatively-run school.

"The main problem concerns the support that we could expect from both students and the San Diego citizenry", Stanford wrote in an editorial in the Explorers' Log in December. Stanford said the move to Point Loma could be successful "...if every student brought a new one with him next fall."

Meanwhile, the School of Business was considering itself one of the best business schools on the West Coast and looked forward to being the best. The school consisted of departments of accounting, marketing, secretarial administration, finance, and general business. A labor-management department was being formulated, and an institute of foreign economic relations was under consideration.

At the same time, the new School of Liberal Arts was within two years of turning out its first graduates. Plans for schools of art, architecture and music were on the drawing boards, while schools of engineering, religion, dentistry and medicine were being considered. All of this of course was being done in the name of service to the citizens of San Diego. It was a cause which forward-thinking San Diegans could embrace.

Good news came at the start of 1950, when the City Council approved the zoning variance Balboa University wanted for the Point Loma property. But with it came the bad news that the estate was tied up with tax problems that had to be settled with the Bureau of Internal Revenue before negotiations could proceed.

And at the same time the State Bar of California dropped a 302-page bomb on the law school in the form of a survey board report entitled "Survey of Legal Education". To some it appeared to be a case of prejudice in favor of graduates of the law schools of the largest universities in the state, including U.C.L.A., U.C. at Berkeley, U.S.C. and Stanford, against the graduates of the law schools of the smaller universities.

It was also a cause for further financial pressure. The report recommended that provisional accreditation be extended to Balboa, pending approval by the American Bar Association. On February 28, President Stanford reported in his "From the President's Desk" column in the *Explorers' Log* that "negotiations on the Point Loma site are still at a standstill." Two other sites had been located.

They would be suitable, said Stanford, in case it would become impossible to obtain the one on Point Loma. "It is the feeling of the administration that an attractive campus would immeasurably enhance the prestige of the university."

Simultaneously, a Department of Religion had been established with courses in biblical history, comparative religion, ethics and other such subjects offered on a non-sectarian basis. Classes were to begin with the Spring Quarter.

On June 21, the Class of 1950 was graduated in ceremonies held at the Recital Hall in Balboa Park. The degree of Bachelor of Laws was awarded to James F. Woodall who completed his studies in December of 1949, and, among others, to Richard E. Adams, Milton Fredman,[7] Thurlon E. Taylor, Duane E. Wilson (cum laude) and Adolph Zuber, who finished their studies in March, 1950.

Also graduated were Radelle D. Carlson, Hugo M. Fisher,[8] Constantine J. Kardaras, Joseph M. Nuzum and Herbert Scarholm who finished in June, and Fred M. Barner, Jr., who would finish in September.

---

[7] Milton Fredman became a prominent San Diego attorney and founder of a winery.
[8] Hugo Fisher was one more of the many Balboa alumni to grace the San Diego Superior Court

Elsewhere in the *Explorers' Log*, President Stanford announced "....the present plan is to move (to the new Point Loma campus) in the vacation period between the Summer and Fall Quarters."

"Next year", he added, "the graduation program will probably be given in the Greek Bowl", meaning the amphitheatre on the Point Loma property.

Then Stanford added: "Five years ahead, we should have two thousand students and a million dollar plant."

But if Balboa was to have a student body of 2000, it was a question as to how many of those students would be law students. After thirty-two graduated from the School of Law in 1949, and nineteen in 1950, President Stanford and his trustees looked at the class roll of the Class of 1951 and saw that only twenty-one students were scheduled for graduation, including two September students.

Chapter IV

Theosophical Society and the Move to Point Loma

The sale of the Point Loma property to Balboa University was formalized on September 15, 1950, with classes scheduled to begin on September 26.

While Stanford loaded library books into a flat bed truck which he drove to the new site and unloaded onto shelves he had built himself, his lawyers were at work on the pile of papers that would complete the sale.

First, there was the Grant Deed in which Sarah A. Wood and Rose V. Vollmer granted the Point Loma acreage to Balboa University, subject in addition to the usual restrictions, to the restriction that no portion of one part of the property shall be subdivided prior to August 1, 2000, or of another part prior to August 1, 1955.

The deed also provided that so long as Rose Vollmer lived, no buildings could be constructed within a certain area nor could any buildings already in that area be used as a dormitory, clubroom or any other purpose which might tend to create loud or excessive noises. There was a further unusual restriction: "Vivisection or experimentation upon living creatures for any purpose, excepting only tests upon human beings voluntarily consented by them, shall never be done or permitted upon any portion of the property conveyed hereby."

Then came a Deed of Trust between Balboa University, Southern Title & Trust Company, and Wood and Vollmer, the beneficiaries. Next was the Assignment of Rents in which Balboa University assigned all rents on the property to Wood and Vollmer as further security for the payment of the obligation of $185,000 due them. Also signed on that date was a most curious chattel mortgage from the university to Wood and Vollmer in further security for the moneys owed.

In the Order for Partial Distribution of the Estate of George W. Wood to his widow it was indicated that there were twenty-five houses on the former Theosophical Institute property. The chattel mortgage given as further security to Sarah Wood and Rose Vollmer, however, was a six page document with a twenty-three page inventory apparently listing the contents of far more than twenty-five houses.

Inventory in thirty-nine houses is listed, with houses designated by numbers as high as 270 (but they apparently were not numbered consecutively), plus inventories in numbered apartments, rooms, office buildings, an academy, a temple crypt, storerooms and a shack. For each house or other building there were described furniture and fixtures in living rooms, bedrooms, bathrooms, kitchens, basements, hallways, porches, offices and storerooms.

The chattel mortgage listed every conceivable item of furniture, household goods, fixtures and equipment, such as desks, chairs, beds, springs, mattresses, pads, pillows, rugs, water heaters, mirrors, shelves, gas ranges, towel racks, curtains and drapes, congoleum rugs, linoleum, lamps and lamp shades, floor heaters, davenports, book cases, dining tables, ice boxes, refrigerators, picnic tables, hot plates, dishes, garbage cans, mops, cooking utensils, bedspreads, Venetian blinds, even cement mixers, lavatories and plumbing parts!

The inventory lists attached to that chattel mortgage provide a glimpse into the activities and the campus of the Raja Yoga school which had been operated by the Theosophical Society on Point Loma from about 1900 to 1942.

The word theosophy is derived from the Greek (God) and sophia (wisdom), translated most commonly as *divine wisdom*. During the last quarter of the nineteenth century, Darwin's theory of evolution seemed to challenge religion and the spiritual. Many people turned more strongly to the orthodox Christian church, but the time was also inviting to Christian Science, to spiritualism and even to the occult. Mary Baker Eddy's *Science and Health with Key to the Scriptures* was published in 1875, and the Theosophical Society was founded in the same year by a Russian woman, Helena Petrovna Blavatsky.

The objectives of the Society were to provide a comparative study of religions, philosophies and sciences, to investigate the unexplained laws of nature and the powers latent in man, to disseminate a knowledge of the sublime teachings of that pure esoteric system of the archaic period, and to aid in the institution of the Brotherhood of Humanity.[9]

Born in 1847 in Massachusetts, Katherine Tingley spent years away from home, had two early unsuccessful marriages, first swore by spiritualism and then broadened her horizons to occult philosophies of Eastern origin, and rose from obscurity to head the world Theosophical Society in 1900.

She had cared for Civil War wounded as a teenager, and she had operated the Do-Good Mission on the East Side of New York. There she had met William Quan Judge, vice-president of the Theosophical Society, and received a gospel which professed to explain why some people were blessed in life whereas others labored under sordid conditions. "It taught that a man's circumstances, good or bad, were largely the result of his own actions in this life or in a previous one. But having sowed the wind and reaped the whirlwind, he did not need to despair. By patiently enduring his just lot, or karma, and doing good in order to lighten the karmic load, he might ultimately lift himself to a happier existence in this life and in others to come. Here was not just a second chance, but a third, a fourth, or as many as necessary."[10]

During the Spanish-American War, Katherine Tingley organized the Sisters of Compassion and the Relief Committee of the Interna-

---

[9] Charles J Ryan, *H.P. Blavatsky and the Theosophical Movement* and Emmett A. Greenwalt *California Utopia: Point Loma: 1897-1942*

[10] Ibid. *California Utopia*

tional Brotherhood League, commonly called the War Relief Corps. Ultimately, in 1900, having gained leadership of the Society, she was able to establish the Point Loma school which had long been her dream.

The Raja Yoga school, named with the Sanskrit term meaning "royal union", was intended by Mrs. Tingley to provide "the perfect balance of all the faculties, physical, mental and spiritual."[11] It started with five children and within ten years reached its maximum of three hundred. The tuition was similar to that of good private schools, with higher charges for the wealthy to help pay for the poor. The children lived at the school, separated from their parents at an early age, the practice which may have caused the school the most criticism.

Financed by such men as A.G. Spalding, the sporting goods magnate, Walter T. Hanson, a Bibb Manufacturing Company executive, Clark Thurston, head of American Screw Company, and E. August Neresheimer, a wealthy diamond broker, and with the help of Gottfried de Purucker, who succeeded Mrs Tingley in operating the school, the Point Loma land was purchased and extensive construction achieved.

The Raja Yoga school took over a three-storey hotel-sanitarium built earlier on the Point Loma land by Dr. Lorin Wood, an enterprising theosophist, and the inner patio of the building was topped with a huge dome of aquamarine glass. Three lesser domes of other-colored glass were built on towered corners of the building, and it became known as the Homestead.

West of the Homestead was built the most beautiful structure of all, known as the Temple, and crowned by an enormous dome of amethyst-colored glass. There were soon built clusters of round, canvas-topped white wooden framed cottages about 30 feet in diameter, later rebuilt with glass skylights as pinnacles. There was also a row of tents, called Camp Karnak for an Egyptian motif, and most enduring of all, the first Greek Theater in America.[12]

---

[11] *The Voice of the Soul* (Point Loma, 1928)

[12] California Western Law School graduations were held in that magnificent outdoor setting as long as the school was on Point Loma.

Later the handsome white Spalding residence, also glass-domed, and a nine-hole golf course, as well as an imposing Roman gate with a sentinel's box, and an Egyptian gate leading to Camp Karnak were added. As time went on, there were extensive vegetable gardens, cultivated flowers, ornamental trees and fruit orchards, quiet paths and numerous playing fields. There were classes in music, drama and dance, literature and philosophy, archeology and art, as well as all the standard courses common to other schools of the time.

The Point Loma venture, known as the Hill, was truly a community or a colony as well as a school. In addition to the teaching and studies in horticulture, Mrs. Tingley believed that manual labor had special values as a religious or philosophical discipline. There were unsuccessful efforts to manufacture silk from silkworm cocoons, but better results with a bee farm and substantial honey production, as well as decorated china and the ancient batik process of dyeing fabric. The making of uniforms also became a valuable work, and there were a lumber yard, plumbing, blacksmith, paint and machine shops.

The Theosophical Publishing Company had its own press, a book bindery, and printing, photograph and engraving departments. It produced beautifully printed periodicals, essays, propaganda tracts and pamphlets, as well as many books, including the printing and binding of Katherine Tingley's five books.

In 1919, the Theosophical University was organized "to receive maturing Raja Yoga pupils, and by 1928 it had been accredited by the United States Department of Labor as an institution of learning where foreign students could study as nonquota immigrants."[13]

After the death of Katherine Tingley in 1929, Gotttfried de Purucker led the Theosophical Society, the name Raja Yoga was dropped in favor of Lomaland School, uniforms were abandoned, women were allowed to bob their hair, and the rule of silence was waived. The many activities of the Hill were slowly diminished, financial problems escalated with the depression, and the physical beauty of the Hill faded badly. The plays and musical extravaganzas

---

[13] *California Utopia, p.93*

grew less frequent, the gardens withered from lack of water. The huge glass domes of the Academy and the Temple became a danger as the result of continued vibrations from the naval practice firing off the coast, pinnacle ornaments were removed, but vibrations even loosened panes of glass in their lead fittings.[14]

In 1932-33, the Society gave up paying interest on its bond issue and defaulted on taxes. By 1942, unable any longer to maintain the buildings or the grounds and worried about its substandard housing and exposure to increasing military and naval activity on adjacent Federal land, Purucker was forced to abandon the Hill. He had managed, however, to save the Society and take its survivors to a smaller more modern campus. He acquired the site of the California Preparatory School for Boys in Covina, California, where taxes were a third less and water rates two-thirds less.[15] Much of the furniture and fixtures in many of the houses and other buildings must have been left behind, as appears from the extent and variety of the goods and movables described earlier as being contained in the chattel mortgage securing the sellers of the property to Balboa University.

The Hill had been purchased from the Theosophical Society by George W. Wood, a Coronado man who intended to dispose of the land and buildings to the Federal Housing Authority to accommodate as many as five thousand people. He had rented out many of the small houses, but the planning authorities, because of the condition of the buildings, limited occupancy to three hundred.[16] It was after Wood's death that Dwight Stanford was able to negotiate the purchase of the property from his heirs.

The task of changing the Point Loma campus from that of the abandoned Theosophical Institute's University and Raja Yoga school to the Balboa University campus was an imposing one. The many residential houses were hardly adaptable to university use, although an administration building was. Likewise, the handsome outdoor amphitheatre was most suitable for stage presentations and ideal for

---

14 Ibid. p..200
15 Ibid. p. 205
16 Ibid. p..206

unique and beautiful commencement exercises. Many buildings had to be razed and new ones built.

The remodeling of the new campus went ahead in earnest with Dr. Max Lund, Dean of the Liberal Arts School, as the principal foreman. But Balboa University, the former Balboa Law School, just wasn't the same. The only thing about it which was still the same was that there were debts and cash flow problems. What was very different from the fledgling night law school was that the amount of money which had to be borrowed to stay even with the debts and cash flow problems was far greater. (But they couldn't even dream what cash flow problems would be for its successor USIU some twenty years later!).

As the 1950-51 school year wore on, President Stanford reached a decision. He would step aside as president and assume the role of Chairman of the Board of Trustees.

The Explorers' Log for March 13 carried the news of the appointment of Dr. Robert W. Griffin as Balboa's third president. Griffin was a Chula Vista educator and business administrator. His Ph.D. was from the University of California in education. Both Griffin and Mrs. Griffin were active in various programs of the Methodist Church and he was a former president of the Board of Trustees of the First Methodist Church of San Diego.

Dr. Griffin had been president and general manager of the Griffin Lumber Company, president of the El Rey Investment Corporation, secretary and general manager of the Mar Vista Investment Corporation, and president and general manager of the South Bay Mortgage and Investment Company. At one point in his career, he had been an associate editor and reading consultant to Reader's Digest.

He assumed office with the university on July 1, just as the Class of 1951 was about to be graduated. Bachelor of Laws degrees went, among others, to Earl James Cantos[17], Paul Duke, June Dolores Hastings, Barbara Lange Hayes, Lyle G. Kunz, Edward Cadwallader Pitts, Almon R. Reisweber, Sunshine A. Summers, and Raymond

---

[17] Earl Cantos was another in Balboa's long list of San Diego judges

Winters. Paul V. Pierik and John G. Ronis[18] were the September graduates.

A chilling campus bulletin, one of the first issued in the regime of the new president, appeared on July 11. It said:

"All law students who are within approximately one quarter of graduation submit a list of courses and units needed. This is necessary in order that a Fall schedule may be planned. Please submit this information to the Office of Admissions not later than August 1st."

When the Board of Trustees met in mid-August, the grim decision was made to suspend operation of the law school. Although remaining a Board member, Dwight Stanford resigned in protest from his post as chairman.

Griffin called the ten or twelve law school seniors into his office for a meeting to discuss their academic futures with them. Some accepted the offer of Stanford and Earl Conyers to tutor them with the vague promise that Balboa would grant them degrees. Some transferred to other schools.

Griffin, in making his announcement to the Explorers' Log, emphasized the bright promise of the future for the other parts of the university. The Department of Business Administration was to become the School of Business Administration and the College of Letters, Arts and Sciences was to become the College of Liberal Arts. Bachelors and Masters degrees would be offered in each college, and additional graduate degrees would be offered as soon as possible.

But although the bold headline in the Explorers' Log said: **Suspension Means Suspension Not Cancellation**, nothing could mask the fact that the School of Law, which had been the first school and keystone of the university, was no more.

---

[18] John Ronis later founded a prominent law firm

Chapter V

Balboa Law School in Darkness

Balboa University underwent many changes during the years of its law school's darkness. The student newspaper, *Explorer's Log*, had reported some months before the suspension of the law school, that the university had grown "from Hillcrest and no campus to Point Loma and the finest potential campus on the Pacific Coast". The university was changing with the times, but changes did not always come easily.

Gone was the pre-War era when only a minority of men and a comparative handful of women could hope to get a college education. The promise of the post-War era, where the millions who had served their country could receive an education through the GI Bill of Rights, continued in the early fifties even as the Korean conflict began to flare up. Many believed that soon it would be the few, not the many, who did not have a higher education in the United States.

It was a time for educational institutions to change. That meant that the educators, administrators and board members involved with them would have to change. Some could. Others fell by the wayside.

Growth was now the thing. It was time to think big. It was time for Balboa not to think of itself as a local commuter university but as a university that could be an important factor on a national level—and a short time later even international!

In July of 1951, Robert M. Griffin was inaugurated in the Greek Theatre on Point Loma as president of the university. In October, President Griffin appeared before a meeting of officials of the Southern

41

California-Arizona Methodist Conference to ask that Balboa be adopted as a Methodist university.

The presentation went well. Bishop James C. Baker named the Reverend Kenneth Carlson of Santa Monica to be chairman of a seven-member study committee. The wheels were in motion, but they would turn slowly. The Reverend Carlson was given until the conference's next annual meeting, scheduled for the following June, to make his report.

The Regional Conference was only one of the bodies that had to approve making Balboa the second Methodist institution of higher learning in California—in addition to the College (now University) of the Pacific in Stockton. The Methodist Board of Education and the church's University Senate also had to approve.

In November of 1951, Balboa announced Phase I of a building drive which was to raise $175,000 to renovate existing buildings to accommodate 200 boarders by September, 1952.

But that was only a minor part of the Big Program, which was to raise seven million dollars for new construction to include an administration building, library, chapel, dormitories, little theater, student union, gymnasium, field house, auditorium, music and fine arts building, science building, infirmary, and two academic buildings. (The old Tingley mansion had already become the administration building after Dwight Stanford had proudly announced that the new campus boasted a "Greek Theatre for outdoor assemblies, performances and ceremonies, a beach for swimming and picnicking, and several buildings which can be converted into classrooms and offices.")

Balboa University was on a growth course. It was either grow or collapse. Board members who had no stomach for the dictates of growth—fund-raising and passing sky-high budgets—either bailed out or were otherwise tossed aside.

The Board of Trustees that Dwight Stanford had assembled went through a shakeup. Admiral Frederick C. Sherman, U.S.N. (Ret) had become chairman, and several new trustees were added. Stanford remained a trustee despite his resignation as chairman in protest of the law school's closing. Mrs. Spencer H. Higgins was put in charge of a new women's committee, and George A. Scott, the Walker-Scott department store founder, was named vice-chairman and also headed a newly-created Balboa University Committee. John M. Cranston, a leading San Diego attorney, partner in a large and prestigious law firm, who was to play such an important part in the affairs of the university and the law school for many years, was appointed to the chairmanship of a Balboa University Committee of the San Diego Council of Churches.

Meanwhile in the staff area, a new breed of educator began to emerge. Such an educator was William C. Rust, Ph.D., who was given the unique title of Executive Dean in January, 1952.

"We are exceedingly fortunate to have secured the services of a man with Dr. Rust's background," said President Griffin in announcing Rust's appointment to the newly-created position.

Rust was educated at Methodist DePauw University in Greencastle, Indiana. He did his graduate work at the University of Southern California where he received his doctorate. An ordained minister of the Methodist Church, he had taught at USC and at the Illiff School of Theology. And as would soon be seen, he also had abilities as a fund raiser.

As part of Balboa University's reorganization and expansion plan, the new executive dean was to be responsible for the academic program. Dr. Rust held the academic rank of Professor of Philosophy.

William C. Rust was a remarkable man. He was a visionary and a BIG thinker, and pleased to be part of an institution where the prevailing thought was to shift gears and move forward. At times he could have the fervor and intensity of an evangelist preacher and the idealism of a high-school graduate, at others the hard salesmanship and subterfuge of a huckster of patent-medicines. His ultimate career as the president of the university spanned some forty years of brilliance and error, real estate acquisitions and sales, confusion, turmoil, accomplishments and defeats, hirings and firings, campus openings and closings.

But above all, as president, Dr. Rust had an abiding conviction that he was destined to lead a new kind of university, dedicated to true scholarship, morality and international understanding, and he devoutly believed that such a university must have a law school. So it was that in 1958 he brought the university's law school back to life—and indeed it was his even greater commitment to academic excellence which permitted him seventeen years later to sacrifice the university's best interests to the law school's true renaissance as an independent institution. However, we are jumping far ahead of the story.

As executive dean of the university, Rust's first move was to establish the Community College, an expansion of afternoon and evening classes, with programs leading toward the Bachelor of Science, Bachelor of Arts, and Bachelor of Business Administration degrees. Rust added "Director of Community College" to his executive dean title.

"There is." said President Griffin, "a widespread need for the services of a high type college-level program designed for the mature student who desires a college education. The Community College of Balboa University offers a curriculum concerned with the development of ideals, acquisition of college-level techniques, knowledge and an understanding interdependence of people."

Meanwhile, things began to pop with the Methodist Church. Not waiting for the annual meeting in June, Reverend Carlson's special committee on acquiring Balboa University made its report at another meeting in Los Angeles. The committee recommended that the Methodist Conference accept Balboa, but only after several extremely stringent financial prerequisites had been achieved.

According to Griffin, the money needed to meet the conditions demonstrating community support, providing new facilities and endowment, as well as an operating income fund, totaled $2,350,000. He announced that the first campaign for the funds would open in July.

Before the fund-raising got underway, Balboa changed its name to California Western University. Admiral Sherman made the announcement on May 31, 1952, saying that an expanded program was contemplated for the following school year.

"This is not just another school with an assortment of standard courses," he said, "but a university with courses tailored to meet the needs of this day and hour—a training program for successful living, a bold effort in the development of dynamic leadership."

The program, he added, "will be centered on the premise that the greatest need of our world is leadership in the area of human relations." These words might well have emanated from Dr. Rust, and exactly what was meant by them would be shown in course announcements to follow later.

At the time of the announcement, it was noted that the university had a student body of 250. It was intended to put dormitories and a dining hall into operation in September so enrollment could be increased to 400.

A week later, the San Diego *Union's* education writer came back with a notebook full of ponderous announcements by Griffin which were dutifully published along with photographs. "California Western University," he wrote, "will be devoted to a philosophy of education as old as the roots of western culture."

The school was described as "San Diego's newest institution of higher learning on the Point Loma grounds once occupied by the Theosophical Institute," a nice phrase which allied the school with San Diego's roots while ignoring the struggles and the accomplishments of Balboa Law School, Balboa College, and Balboa University.

Balboa stood for all that was provincial, old-fashioned, and somehow regrettable. The new California Western University, said President Griffin, went back for its inspiration to Oxford and Cambridge, and even to the Athenian groves where Socrates walked with his students!

"California Western," its president said, would not offer "a narrow training in a technique or a profession" such as the law. Instead, he said, "we have a program that will develop an insight into our society. It will seek to impart education, understanding."

According to Griffin, two basic characteristics would make California Western into "a university that would turn out well-rounded, educated men and women." One was the core curriculum, and the other was "a close association of students and professors." The core curriculum was largely the work of Dr. Rust, Griffin said. "Its closest parallel is the curriculum of Brandeis University."

Core curriculum meant that all students would be required to take certain basic courses "which unites subject matter from several formal learning disciplines." One first-year course cited as an example was "Development of Civilization."

The idealistic, if not grandiose, plan was to have four professors do the teaching, each on a different day of the week. One was to treat the subject from the standpoint of philosophy and religion, a second was to bring in history and political science, and the third day's professor would look at the subject from the point of view of sociology and anthropology.

On the fourth day the professor would view the progress of civilization as expressed in the development of fine arts. On the fifth day, a symposium would be held, featuring all of the professors. Griffin's folksy but starry-eyed explanation was: "The idea appealed to me because of my experience with what I call 'cafeteria education.' It was not until the last session of my undergraduate career that I had a course which synthesized the various unconnected courses I had taken. Many students never have such a course. I believe that education should start out with one."

The last graduation exercises of the Balboa Law School were held in the Greek Theatre on the Point Loma campus on July 12, 1952. Bachelor of Law degrees were awarded to fifteen graduates.

The Southern California-Arizona Methodist Conference debated at its annual meeting whether or not to make California Western a Methodist university. After three hours of discussion, it voted in favor with the condition that the school would have to meet the financial conditions of Reverend Carlson's special committee.

Robert M. Griffin resigned as president on October 6, 1952, saying he wanted to safeguard his health from undue stress (although it was also reported that several trustees had met at the Cuyamaca Club to ask for his resignation because they disagreed with his policies). Thus ended a brief but busy (if not stormy) twenty-month tenure. Dr. Griffin had guided the reorganization of the old Balboa University into the new California Western, brought William Rust on board, and had taken the important first steps that would lead to the relatively short affiliation with the Methodist Church—but he had presided over the closing or "suspension"of Balboa Law School, which had been the original school of the university!

Also under Griffin's regime, four campus buildings were restored and an additional 23 acres of Point Loma property were acquired, bringing the school's total acreage to 120.

William Rust was appointed interim executive head of the university and was confirmed as president at a meeting of the Board of Trustees at the end of November. The announcement was made by Admiral Sherman, saying: "We feel he is exceptionally well qualified to guide the growth of a university which will expand with the community." Except for Admiral Sherman's announcement, the beginning of Rust's administration received little public attention.

In January of 1954, under a banner headline in the *Union*, the university announced a fund drive for a mere $178,000, significantly less than the seven million fund drive announced in November, 1951, or the drive for $2,230,000 launched in the summer of 1952!

Chairman Edmund T. Price said the money was needed for necessary improvements and to wipe out indebtedness. What a harbinger of the future!

Perhaps inadvertently, it was revealed that the university had not grown as well as had been hoped a year or two before. Enrollment was said to be at 230 students. Less than two years earlier, in announcing the name change from Balboa to California Western, Admiral Sherman had said enrollment was at 250 with the hope of increasing it to 400 the next year.

In announcing the quest for $178,000, the fund-raisers pushed all the buttons they could, not excluding the panic button, at a civic meeting at the El Cortez Hotel. Price, as chairman, tried to induce a little worry into his listeners: "Within a few short years, we in the San Diego area will be faced with the problem of providing adequate facilities for a considerably increased number of students ready for college education."

"Our objective," he said, "will be a student body of 800 undergraduate and 400 graduate students. In terms of the local economy, that will mean an annual income of about $1,500,000 from student fees, property and perhaps church support."

Rust followed Price to the podium to say that California Western had reduced its indebtedness by $100,000 in the previous year and had made "big advancements" in its scholastic standing. Yet another harbinger of the future. That was not to be the last time that Rust would be heard to talk about "reducing indebtedness" and "advancements in scholastic standing!"

Dr. Malcolm A. Love, president of San Diego State College, further defined the problem raised by Price. "In 1962 there will be two and one-half times as many college students here as there are now, and by 1968 there will be a further increase of 150 per cent."

The problem, he said, would come about because of the many newcomers to San Diego and because the city had only three colleges: California Western, the San Diego College for Women, and San Diego State. Campaign co-chairman Robert J. Sullivan stressed the importance of building a local university because "many parents cannot afford to send students out of town for a college education."

Ewart W. Goodwin, the other campaign co-chairman, stressed what might be called a Chamber of Commerce angle: "From an economic standpoint, 800 students mean as much to the community as 400 skilled workers. They mean approximately a million dollars a year. Therefore, within fifteen years, whatever money we invest in California Western will bring back at least fifteen million dollars to San Diego."

Dr. Ralph Daillard, superintendent of city schools, added to the definition of the need when he said that within a few years 250 per cent more students would be ready for college.

Then it was time to pass the hat. Chairman Price announced that George A. Scott had called from Florida to pledge $10,000. Price, Goodwin and trustee Harold B. Starkey pledged $2000 each. Price said he would ask Solar directors to subscribe an additional $6000.

Before the meeting ended, Admiral Sherman put in a pitch for free enterprise, reminding the gathering that California Western was a non-tax-supported university representing free enterprise in education.

John M. Cranston, who had been secretary of the Board when Dr. Rust was installed as president, was completely taken by the new president and his charming wife, Rosemary. A devout Methodist whose brother was the first dean of the School of Religion at Clairemont College, Cranston urged the affiliation with the Methodist Church, feeling the denominational backing would make the school stronger. He was joined in this feeling by George Warner, Sr., pastor of San Diego's first Methodist Church, as well as Bishop Randolph Phillips, who wanted San Diego to have a Methodist College in the image of schools like Emory, Southern Methodist, Northwestern, Syracuse, Puget Sound and Willamette.

California Western University became affiliated with the Methodist Church in 1956, although it is doubtful that the financial prerequisites of Reverend Carlson's special committee were ever actually met.

Reports of the effects and benefits of that affiliation, which lasted only ten years, are sparse and most varied. To begin with, the power to name the trustees was given to the Methodist Conference. For some time the Conference accepted whatever new trustees the existing Board wanted, and matters ran somewhat smoothly.

However, the Methodist financial contributions to the university soon became the chief cause of friction. It was reported that although the Methodists sought more control, they did not provide sufficient monetary assistance to satisfy the university's needs. One example given was the Campus and Church Crusade, a drive through the

Conference to raise one million dollars for the university and more for the church. Dr. Rust reported that he spent much of his time for an entire year to try to find the money, and it was eventually raised—whereupon the Conference did provide the university with a million dollars. Dr. Rust reported, however, that that sum was insufficient even to cover over a million dollars paid out by the university in scholarships to Methodist students.

By 1966, a group of Methodists wanted more power and the right to name to the Board of Trustees people the university did not want. On the university board at that time were some of San Diego's biggest hitters: Fred Rohr, the aircraft parts maker, Walter Zable, founder of Cubic Corporation, Bob Walter, a major real estate player, Claude Ryan, the airplane builder, Morley Golden, leading building contractor, George Peck, top automobile dealer, Irving Salomon, outstanding philanthropist, and John Cranston, one of the city's top attorneys. The university had worked out a major acquisition from the United States government of the former Camp Elliott, north of San Diego, which would make an ideal large university campus. Title to the property was taken in the name of a separate corporation, of which the above-named group were the trustees, without the Methodist members of the California Western board.

Upon the decision to disaffiliate, at a meeting of the California Western board, these board members pointed out that unless the disaffiliation was agreed to without any problems for the university, they would all resign from the board and withdraw all of their financial support, leaving the university with its enormous debts for the Methodists to contend with. Faced with that prospect, the disaffiliation took place.

Thereupon the new corporation was merged into California Western, and the university owned and controlled both the Point Loma campus and the Elliott property.

With respect to the effects on the university of the Methodist affiliation, in retrospect it certainly does appear that either because of that affiliation or because of the individual beliefs and vision of Drs. Griffin and Rust and many members of the Board of Trustees, the university (and indeed the law school) had an aura of morality and orthodoxy not typical of many universities. Especially during the turbulent years of dissent and confrontation on so many American campuses, the California Western campus remained orderly, calm and quiet!

Chapter VI

Rebirth as California Western School of Law

As rebirths go, this was fairly tranquil. The reopening of the Balboa University Law School, renamed the California Western University School of Law, took place in the fall of 1958, in a building owned by Morley Golden at 1729 Fifth Avenue, a few blocks north of downtown San Diego.

Eight students showed up for the first classes.

Dr. Rust named Lloyd C. Swortwood, director of the California Western School of Business since its inception at the same address on Fifth Avenue, as dean of the law school. Both an attorney and a certified public accountant, Swortwood held a Bachelor of Science degree from Catholic DePaul University and a Juris Doctor degree from Northwestern University. The plan was to offer a three-year course to full-time day students leading to the Bachelor of Law degree.

Trustee John Cranston headed the Advisory Board of the school that assisted Swortwood in formulating a curriculum and choosing a faculty. Others on the Advisory Board were Superior Court Judges Ault, Toothaker and Turrentine, and attorneys Robert Conyers, James Focht, Charles Burch, Fred Lindley, Paul Pierik, Jack Harrison, Charles Holliday, Frank Pomerantz, Edgar Luce, Jr., E.G. Merrill, and Brooks Crabtree.[19]

The faculty under Dean Swortwood included a mixture of retired professors and novices. Among these was John Bradway, a pioneer in

---

[19] Judge Ault was to play a most important role in the law school, and major contributions were also made by judges Toothaker and Turrentine, as well as Messrs. Focht, Lindley and Conyers, who later became judges.

the Legal Aid Society, whom Dr. Rust recruited to the faculty after he had retired from Duke University. Burke Shartel was a retired professor from the University of Michigan, while Lou Henderson, who served both as librarian and professor, came from the University of Nebraska.

In the first two years of the school's renewed existence, first-year students came from four different colleges and universities to attend school in a building which had three classrooms, two seating thirty students each and one seating twelve. Unfortunately, Balboa's law library had been given away to the University of San Diego which then used it in establishing its new law school in 1954. Opportunely, Dr. Rust was able to cajole the Chicago Bar Association into sending the school a substantial number of law books, and those books provided the core of the law library first available to California Western's eight new students!

Very little is known of the fortunes of the law school during its first two years except that the total enrollment in 1958 and 1959 ultimately increased to twelve. Six students from the group that enrolled at the reopening in 1958 received Bachelor of Law degrees in the first graduating class in 1961.

John Cranston appeared before the conference of Delegates of the State Bar of California urging accreditation of the re-established school, and Dr. Rust began his quest for the monies needed to provide a proper building for the law school on the Point Loma campus. Fred H. Rohr, founder of the Rohr Corporation, was to be the chief source of funds for the new building which was ultimately named for him and Mrs. Rohr. The Moot Court was named as the result of a gift by Mrs. Lena Sefton Clark in memory of her husband, Colonel Henry B. Clark, and the law library was named in recognition of a gift of the San Diego Savings and Loan Association.

Very early on, plans for the design of the building were begun under the direction of architect Richard John Lareau. For some forty years, Lareau was the architect upon whom Dr. Rust relied for the many new and remodeled buildings of the university all over the world. He also became Rust's advisor and confidante.

But until the new building was completed, the law school operated in the cramped quarters on Fifth Avenue shared with the School of Business. The California state accreditation was granted the school in 1961, and provisional accreditation of the American Bar Association was obtained in 1962, confirmed in 1964.

It is not clear whether Dean Swortwood was originally intended to be the permanent dean, or acting dean until the appointment of a permanent dean. Nor are all the facts concerning a very unusual and near-tragic incident involving faculty member Lou Henderson. It is not known whether he was being considered for the deanship, but it is known that he was very seriously injured in an apparent suicide attempt when he fell from an upper floor of the Bank of America building. His fall was broken by landing on a Yellow Cab whose driver was also seriously injured.

At any rate in September of 1960, Robert K. Castetter became dean of the law school upon his appointment by Dr. Rust. In those days at California Western University no consideration or approval of the faculty or anyone but the university president was needed for the appointment of a dean—or indeed even for the appointment of faculty members.

Castetter had come to San Diego State College (now San Diego State University) in 1954 to head its department of Business Law. He was a 1941 graduate of Washington and Jefferson College who became interested in the academic field and the law while on active duty with the military in World War II.

He took his LL.B. degree from Chase College of Law in Cincinnati, Ohio, in 1952, and obtained a Master's degree in law at the University of Indiana just prior to moving to California. It was Castetter upon whom Dr. Rust called to guide the growth of tiny California Western School of Law. By the time he took over in September, 1960, eleven more students had enrolled, making a student body of twenty three.

There was apparently some unrest among the small faculty, along with some departures. The school's next important move was to hire Marvin J. Anderson to teach real property, constitutional and administrative law. Anderson also became faculty advisor for Phi Alpha Delta, one of the two legal fraternities with chapters on the California Western campus.[20] A 1942 graduate of the University of Wisconsin School of Law, Anderson would leave California Western in 1964 to become assistant dean and registrar (later dean) at Hastings School of Law in San Francisco.

Also hired were Bernard Auerbach, a recent graduate of New York University law school, who remained for two years, and Doris Yendes (later Alspaugh), another recent law school graduate. Mrs. Alspaugh had come as the law school's librarian, but taught until 1967, when she left to become associate professor and assistant dean at the law school of the University of San Diego.

In the fall of 1962, retired Marine Brigadier-General James Snedeker, the first of the influential long-term faculty members, was recruited. General Snedeker had been a field officer, had worked on the Uniform Code of Military Justice, and after retirement from the Marine Corps had taught at the University of San Francisco. His quiet air of authority and ethical conduct helped create the conservative atmosphere of the young law school. He was followed by five men who all joined the faculty in 1964.

Professor William Burby was a very widely-known and highly respected law professor who had retired from USC after a long career. Dr. Rust, who invariably thought big and aimed high, insisted that efforts be made to persuade Burby to come to teach at California Western. Ultimately, despite Castetter's reticence, the efforts were made and Burby accepted.

With his erect posture and dignified demeanor, Burby was every inch the traditional law professor, and, along with Professor Bradway, added enormously to the stature of the young school. Burby's full head

[20] On December 4, 1964, Brandeis Inn of Phi Delta Phi was officially installed in ceremonies at the San Diego County Courthouse, followed by a reception and banquet at the Yacht Club on San Diego Bay.

of white hair led him to be known as the "silver fox" by his admiring and respectful students.

Robert Meiners was a Dickinson Law School alumnus and editor of its law review. He held a graduate degree from Harvard, and had also been a fellow at Yale. A tenured professor at the University of Pittsburgh, he had also taught at the USC law school.

John Lindsey, became the law school librarian and important confidante and advisor to Dean Castetter. Lindsey was of great importance in the very early years in organizing a proper law school library, with limited budget, which was acceptable to the American Bar Association and the Association of American Law Schools.

James Leahy, who had been first in his class at the University of North Dakota law school, a member of the state legislature, and the head of a bank trust department, specialized in wills and estates and constitutional law. Leahy became a conscientious constitutional scholar, an outstanding teacher, and sometime administrator as associate dean. Despite having been a Republican legislator in conservative North Dakota, Leahy became an ardent defender of students' rights and disciple of the more liberal opinions of the Supreme Court. He provided an excellent balance to the more conservative views of Snedeker and Lindsey, and later of S. Houston Lay, who joined the faculty in 1967, at the same time as Tom Coyne, a young Indiana law school alumnus.

Samuel M. Chapin had been a name partner in a New York City law firm and was a nationally known labor lawyer. Retired in San Diego, Chapin agreed to teach part time at the law school. He was a quiet, unassuming man who found enormous pleasure in teaching. Although nominally only a part-time faculty member, Chapin gave unstintingly of his time and expertise to his students. He coached the appellate moot court participants and expanded on the early efforts of General Snedeker in establishing a pubescent trial court program, then rare among law schools.

Along with Professor Bradway, Lloyd Swortwood, the first dean, who continued teaching for a time after stepping down as dean, and

Doris Alspaugh, this group was the nucleus of the law school faculty during its early years.

In the fall of 1962, the school was able to leave its dismal quarters with the bare wooden stairways on Fifth Avenue and move into its bright new building on Point Loma overlooking the Pacific Ocean, and in February of 1963, formal dedication ceremonies were held. The school's move to the former home of the Theosophical Institute, was most significant. It somehow tied it to "old San Diego" and its roots. As reported in the San Diego *Union*, "Once upon a time, the fog-enshrouded, chaparral-covered slopes of Point Loma were home to one of the most active learning, cultural and social centers in the United States."

"From the turn of the century until just after the outbreak of World War II, the Universal Brotherhood and Theosophical Society's international headquarters—known as Lomaland—was situated on about 400 acres of peninsula land..." Both a Utopian dream and a daring social experiment with its amalgam of grand white buildings and multi-colored glass domes, it seemed to many as an early quasi-religious cult. Nevertheless, after a period of skepticism by San Diegans, Lomaland gained increasing acceptance, and by the 1920's, its facilities were seen by tourists on guided bus tours. Even representatives of government, as well as leaders in the fields of literature, the arts, and science from all over the world, came to lecture or visit.

There can be no doubt that the presence of the law school amidst the towering cypress and eucalyptus, the groves of pepper trees and the scattered pines, planted by the hundreds on the previously barren landscape by the Theosophists, had a profound effect on students and faculty alike. So also did the "Statement of Policies and Regulations" of the university. The Point Loma campus truly seemed, in the turbulent sixties and early seventies, to be a tranquil island, a campus like those in the college movies of handsome clean-cut letter-sweatered football heroes and pert, blonde bobby-soxed cheerleaders!

In early 1964, President Rust had stopped off at Pittsburgh while en route from New York to San Diego. He had scheduled an employment interview with Robert Meiners. The interview took place at an airline ticket counter.

"We do not permit faculty members to drink with students," Rust told Meiners. It was a moment before Meiners said: "I can live with that." That short interview was evidence also of Rust's common practice of flying at night on university business and so saving hotel bills.

On the same junket, Dr. Rust had summoned Jim Leahy from his home in North Dakota to meet him at a Kansas City hotel. Rust wanted to know if Leahy could teach at the law school without attempting to convert his students to Roman Catholicism.

"I'll try not to, sir," was Leahy's reply.

The university policies and regulations contained references to "decent, wholesome campus life", selection and retention of students with "emphasis not only upon academic ability but also upon personality, character traits and attitudes", and to "Bodily cleanliness, appropriate dress, and orderly living conditions...to set the desired tone of campus climate."Alcohol, firearms, drugs, and smoking in all public areas were prohibited. There were special regulations respecting neatness of dress, grooming, and shoes or footwear in all university buildings except dormitory rooms.

The university handbook of the time also provides an insight into the university and its policies. The handbook stated that the *president* had the power to hire, discharge and fix the salaries of the academic and administrative staffs and other employees within the overall salary budget approved by the Board of Trustees.

Today, of course, the faculty and the dean in all graduate schools are much more actively involved in hiring, discharging and the fixing of salaries. In no accredited schools can anyone be hired without faculty recommendation by a two-thirds majority at least, and no faculty member may be retained without a similar vote. Likewise, no faculty member is granted tenure without the recommendation of a consensus of the faculty.

The university on Point Loma's handbook defined the term faculty of the School of Law as being composed not only of the full-time faculty members of the law school, but also of the dean of the law school and the president of the university. That body was given responsibility for participating in the development of academic programs with recommendations to be made through the dean to the president!

Already looking forward to his dream of colleges in several countries providing curricula which would allow the free interchange of credits and of movement, Dr. Rust believed his autocracy, as opposed to faculty governance, was essential—and often caused problems for him with deans, faculty and accrediting agencies.

The net effect of the university regulations and this autocratic approach—and his complete command of the budget—was that the law school was substantially dominated and controlled by President Rust.

The handsome new law school building, however, situated as it was with its unlimited vista of the Pacific, and somewhat away from most of the other campus buildings, did make it easier for the law school to operate as a separate entity from the rest of the university. Primarily on one floor and built around a small courtyard into and across which all the faculty and students had to pass going to or from classrooms, the library or offices, there was a remarkable feeling of closeness and camaraderie. Only the moot court was not on the ground floor.

There was also a so-called Model Attorney's Lounge facing the courtyard, which along with the dean's office, had been furnished (far better than the other rooms) through the generosity of Reverend Clark McElmury, who gave the invocation and benediction at the law school commencements for more than twenty years.[21]

The cost of the new law school building was variously reported to have been $128,000 and $143,000, and one T. A. Stanfield was the contractor. It is reported that Mr. Stanfield died before the construction was completed, but that his wife fulfilled the contract.

---

[21] McElmury was the first one to agree many years later (even before I was able to obtain officers' and trustees' liability insurance) to be a trustee of the then newly-independent law school after I'd explained its purchase to him.

Decorating the front of the law school, on the side facing the sea, was a bold contemporary sculpture pictured prominently in all early law school publications. The noted southern California artist, James Hubbell, at architect Richard Lareau's urgent recommendation, had been commissioned to do the work. [22]

Since 1968, the law school of which I am writing has been an integral part of my life. Since that year there is little concerning the school in which I have not participated or been intimately acquainted. The full story of the first ten years of its rebirth, however, while very near in time to my first joining it, must come from various more or less reliable sources—as indeed must most history.

Through high school and the first two years of college, I accepted as immutable truth whatever was told me as "history" and whatever appeared in history books. It was in college that it first occurred to me that "history" is not truth handed down to us by oracles, but is in reality simply information gleaned from documents and their interpretation and observations and perceptions of people. The accuracy of that information depends upon many variables just as does the accuracy of the recording of the information. The biases and prejudices of the actors, the extent of their intimacy with the events in which they claim to have participated are sometimes known, often are not. Also the biases and prejudices of those who analyze and report the information provided by the "participants" add yet another variable to the accuracy of the "history."[23]

It is only as I have gotten older and have had occasion to read so-called "history" of events in which I participated or which occurred during my lifetime that I have come to see how much difference there can be in the perception of the same events. When I read in college about World War I (then only eighteen years in the past!), at first I accepted as absolute fact all that I read in the "history" books

---

[22] When the school was moved to downtown San Diego, I had the sculpture removed in an effort to preserve it. Unfortunately, no suitable location for it could be found and it was ultimately lost.

[23] A quotation appearing in a showcase in front of the main Cleveland Public Library was always intriguing: "The value of a person's opinion is in direct proportion to the extent and accuracy of the facts upon which that opinion is based."

with which we were provided. Then when other "history" books reported the same events or interpreted the documents in a very different light, it began to give me pause. And now, when I read accounts of World War II and when many of the events with which I was closely associated have reached the plateau of being "history," the discrepancies have become more and more obvious.

One is tempted to accept "eye-witness" accounts as gospel until two apparently honest "eye-witnesses" provide diametrically opposite accounts. Likewise one is tempted to accept all "documentary" evidence, indeed all written or printed words, as genuine. As discrepancies are found it becomes clear why lawyers place such emphasis on original documents and the "chain of custody" of all documents, and place such reliance on cross-examination.

When eye-witnesses report on events, orally or in writing, there is rarely the opportunity to cross-examine as to their alcohol use the night before, how long they had slept, where they had stood and what they'd been able to see, through whose hands any writings had passed, what animus they had for or against any of the actors, and what if any effect their report had on their income. Likewise, the historians using those reports were not cross-examined as to their biases or prejudices respecting the actors, the reporter, the events or their outcome.

Indeed, even since we have photography, document and sound reproduction, movies and television, unless the reporter or photographer can be subjected to cross-examination, the angles of the shots, the sorts of people interviewed, how many refused to be interviewed, the number of people with different views, the validity and custody of the documents, and the biases of the actors and reporters are still most important variables. And above all have I come to realize that not all writers of non-fiction are historians, and not all historians are good historians or unbiased scholars.

It has been my further observation that we all have one common frailty: we remember our own actions and those of our loved ones as correct, motives as moral, speech as articulate, and feelings as considerate.

How well I remember the first time I read the transcript of a cross-examination I had conducted in a trial. It was impossible for me to understand how the shorthand reporter had mistakenly transformed the beautifully careful and grammatically-worded questions which I had certainly asked into the poorly-worded and halting questions transcribed.

So it is that I have tried to record the facts as accurately as I have been able to perceive them—whether or not they were within my knowledge, and despite the fact that I am certain that my own actions were proper and correct, often even brilliant, my motives ethical and moral, my feelings thoughtful and considerate, and my speech impeccably grammatical!

But to return to the odyssey. A significant event in the law school's early growth was the change from the granting of LL.B. degrees to the conferral of Juris Doctor degrees, as more and more law schools were beginning to do in recognition of the fact that they now all offered three-year programs following four years of college and a required prior B.A. or B.S. degree. Also, in an impressive ceremony, the law school conferred its Juris Doctor on all of the graduates of Balboa Law School, thus providing them with a degree from a fully-accredited law school and bringing them into the fold of California Western alumni.

Shortly after the school had moved to Point Loma, Barbara Costley, the member of the staff who was probably the best known and most loved by all of the students from 1962 until her retirement in 1992, began her work with admissions. She ultimately became the school's Registrar and not only knew every student (and all about them) but attended and in effect presided over every commencement exercise of the school for thirty years. The longevity of her career only slightly exceeded that of Ruth Fuller, who was the dean's secretary from 1962 until 1986.

In 1963, the first student publication of the law school, *La Balanza*, was published. It was in the form of a monthly magazine on glossy paper, well-written, positive and non-confrontational, and was published until 1970, succeeded by the *Commentary*, in newspaper form, which had a checkered history of favorable and unfavorable attitudes, far different from its predecessor.

In 1964, the Student Bar Association (which had been established at the school's rebirth in 1958) adopted a student Code of Ethics which well demonstrates a great difference between the methods and attitudes of today and those of less than forty years ago. The Code then was startlingly simple: "All students of the law school are presumed to be persons of honor, good character, and unquestionable integrity. Accordingly, each student is always expected to conduct himself in a manner that will reflect favorably upon the school and the legal profession."

During the years that I practiced law, the attorneys' Code of Ethics could all be printed in a tiny pamphlet, while the present Code of Professional Responsibility is a long treatise, complete with explanations, containing chapter and verse specifically setting forth every prohibited action and inaction. Similarly, the Code of Ethics of the law students became for years no longer the simple expression of that of 1964, but a long and tortuous explanation of each prohibited action.

The obvious result of such changes was that instead of trying in every way to honor the broad concepts of ethical conduct, specificity created the tendency to skirt or technically avoid the carefully-defined violations—which suggest that if not specifically set forth as wrong, all other actions are proper—as with the statutes of the criminal law!

These changes reflected many societal attitudes. The avowed purpose of the specificity was to avoid discretionary punitive actions, provide complete and specific prohibitions—leaving nothing to interpretation and therefore possible prejudicial enforcement. Only very recently the law school's Code of Ethics has once again avoided that specificity!

It seems to me it had been similar thinking which required the use of numbers on all examinations, intended to hide the identity of the students from their teachers. This is to prevent possible prejudice or discrimination—despite the fact that for the rest of the students' professional lives, every client, every judge and every juror will know who they are!

In 1965, the law school entered the family of fully respectable law schools by establishing a Law Review and publishing its inaugural issue, with Professor Meiners as the faculty advisor, a post in which he served for many years. Only a few years later, under the auspices of Professor Lay, the International Law Journal became a reality with its first issue.

Houston Lay had had a distinguished career in the diplomatic service and was deeply committed to the subject of international law. He wrote extensively in the area, advocated and created a strong international law program and library for the school, and promoted the school's very successful participation in the Jessup International Law Moot Court competition. His student teams and individual team members consistently won high honors for the school.

The law school bulletin for the academic year 1965-1966 contained an amusing error. After enthusing that the university was a privately-endowed co-educational institution affiliated with the Methodist Church, it proudly claimed to be "dedicated to the high ideals of Judo-Christian tradition." The zealous bulletin writer—and the proof-reader—apparently confused the Japanese physical combat system, *Judo* with *Judeo-*!

That law school bulletin also described the California Western University campus as being located on 140 acres of wooded land, while in both the 1949 and 1950 issues of the Balboa University *Explorer*, the campus was proudly described as 97 acres. There were several reports that Robert Griffin, as president of the university, had added 23 acres to the campus during his tenure, bringing it to 120 acres.

Under President Rust, as evidence of his fund-raising abilities, there had been added the Ryan Library (Ryan Aircraft), the Percy H.

Goodwin Memorial Chapel (Goodwin Insurance), Salomon Hall (Colonel Irving Salomon), the Golden Gymnasium (Golden Contractors), John B. Starkey Memorial Science Building (First Federal Savings & Loan), the Rohr law school building, Clark Moot Court and San Diego Savings and Loan law library—as well as 20 acres of land. The precise provenance of those extra 20 acres is not known, but if Mrs. Volmer still owned them, Dr. Rust probably was able to persuade her to give or sell them at a bargain price to the university!

Law school tuition for the school year 1965-1966 was $30 per unit, whether for credit or audited, or $900 per year for the typical 30 units. The application fee was $10, with a library fee of $10. Graduation, including rental of a cap and gown, cost $25. By the end of the century the tuition for the standard two trimester program had grown to $20,500 a year!

A major accomplishment of Dean Castetter and those who worked with him, and a most important advancement in the fortunes and reputation of the law school occurred in December, 1967, when the school became a member of the prestigious Association of American Law Schools.

The chief impediment to admission into the AALS was the law school library, which when inspected in 1965 fell well below the association's standards both as to volume count and seating space for students. At the same time, except for Professor Lindsey, there were no professional library personnel—only eight part-time student assistants.

Fortunately, with excellent reporting, planning and promising—and cajoling of the right Executive Committee members by both Lindsey and Castetter—and promises of larger library budgets from Dr. Rust, the Executive Committee of the AALS was persuaded not to oppose California Western's application for membership. The presence on the faculty of both Professor Bradway and Professor Burby, well-known in academia, was also most helpful, and the General Assembly adopted the ultimate favorable recommendation of the Executive Committee.

Having been begun in 1962, and flourishing throughout the 1960's was the Student Wives' Club, later named the Petti-Court (one can only imagine the scorn in which such an organization, with such a name, would be held today). But at that time there were almost no women students and many of the men were married to women who had been uprooted from some other part of the country, were lonesome, and needed the friendship and support of other student wives and faculty wives.

Marj Castetter, the wife of the dean, was instrumental in the establishment and operation of the Petti-Court, her efforts were deeply appreciated and lauded by the students' wives who participated. Regular meetings were held and refreshments provided, usually at the homes of faculty wives, and speakers were invited to talk and conduct discussions relating to matters of interest to the group.

Both the recollections of participants and photographs in publications of the time reveal that during the law school's earliest years, actually until the very late 1960's, faculty and students alike (and their spouses) were always dressed in dress shoes, jackets, shirts and ties, the women in dresses. The gradual change in dress, first the discarding of the jackets by the students, then the ties, the change from dresses to slacks, from slacks to denims, then less and less formality of dress in the students, and even ultimately among some of the faculty certainly mirrored the changes in all of society.

Whether or not there is any relationship, at the same time as the dress was more formal and less casual, the curriculum was more formal and structured. All of the courses in all three years were shown as required in the 1965-66 Bulletin, except for the availability of up to 6 units (two or three courses) of electives in the two semesters of the third year. More recent bulletins show a required curriculum in the first year only, and only nine required courses in the entire second and third years, leaving room for many more elective courses!

Although it was not readily apparent at the time, the change of the name of the university in 1968 to United States International University, along with the institutional changes for which the new name were appropriate, had a profound effect on the law school. Happily, perhaps even with a fortuitous prescience, the faculty and dean of the law school elected to retain its own name, by which it had been known for ten years. Despite its length and unwieldiness, the school's name became California Western School of Law of United States International University.

President Rust had the vision of an international network of colleges which would allow young men and women to study in other countries and to be exposed to other cultures and so bring peace and understanding to the world. To achieve that vision, he began in the latter half of the 1960's to explore the possibilities of establishing campuses in other countries. He conducted extensive studies and surveys of optimum areas, and then having made tentative choices, proceeded actually to examine locations and seek campus sites.

Often with Robert Dunn, a former Bloomington, Illinois practicing attorney who was Vice President of the university and very close to Dr. Rust, and often with Dick Lareau, the architect, he traveled extensively and tirelessly. With a minimum of luggage and flying at night as usual to save on hotel rooms (a practice in which Dunn and Lareau found little pleasure), he explored Great Britain and France, Japan and Taiwan, Mexico and Hong Kong, South Africa, Kenya and Egypt.

The search in the United Kingdom finally narrowed down to Dropmore Park, near Maidenhead on the Thames, the magnificent estate of the man who had been Prime Minister of England in Revolutionary times. From the beginning, Dick Lareau was taken with the gorgeous chandeliers throughout, the art on the walls and the stately manor furniture. During the negotiations he became terribly disturbed that those chandeliers, the art and the furniture would be excluded.

"Dr. Rust, you must have those fabulous chandeliers, they belong in the building, and the heavy tables and other furniture, probably made for the estate, must be included. And the art—it belongs here. The $250,000 more could easily be recovered from the sale of some of the art! Those frames alone are easily worth $1000 each."

"No, we're an educational institution, we're not in the business of buying and selling art."

Lareau finally prevailed with respect to the chandeliers and some of the magnificent tables (plus some used bedroom furniture) at a fair price. He himself bid at the subsequently-held Sotheby's auction for just two of the many paintings: he had left a written bid of $1000 each before he returned to the United States. They sold for $42,500!

Before and after the purchase, it fell to Lareau to work with the town council and the local and district equivalents of the American zoning and building departments to determine how the central building, with its 30 or more bedrooms, could be converted for school use, and whether an additional building could be built inside the formal garden. Experienced in dealing with such bureaucrats in California, Lareau found them to be little different except for their more elegant and precise English.

Robert Dunn well remembered, after the purchase was consummated, their sitting at dusk in the garden of the estate, in the early part of August. There were no books, no faculty, no school furniture—only Graddon Rolands, the director and the lovely old mansion.

But Dr. Rust had directed that the school open on September 22, and some twenty-five students arrived a few days early in happy anticipation. Rolands arranged for them to be taken on a conducted bus tour of Scotland while frantic arrangements were made to rent furniture, assemble a faculty, and acquire some books!

Miraculously, before September ended, the impossible had been accomplished. The school was ready and operations began.

However, after long delays and endless efforts to satisfy the concerns of the town council regarding the need to add a school building in the formal garden area of the estate, Dr. Rust grew restless and determined to sell Dropmore Park.

He had found Ashdown Park, a former training facility for nuns, which was for sale by the Catholic Church. He was able to sell Dropmore to the brother of the Sheikh of Dubai at slightly more than it cost. The purchase of Ashdown, with its fabulously beautiful private chapel, and the complete move of students, faculty and equipment were accomplished without incident.

But the operations of the college in England were never smooth. Almost casually, after some five years at Dropmore and Ashdown, Rust one day told Dunn that there was some problem there and he should go over and straighten it out.

Arrived on the campus, Dunn found much more than "some problem". The faculty, including the director, and all of the employees were members of a most militant union and were on strike because of a letter Rust had written to a history professor. Rust's letter had said that the professor's contract would not be renewed because of his having been drinking on campus. (Somewhat typical of Rust, he had told Dunn nothing of this before he asked him to go to England.)

When Dunn called a meeting of the faculty, they invited their union agent who kept interrupting Dunn whenever he tried to speak, saying there would be no talking until Rust's letter was rescinded. It soon became apparent to Dunn that the problems were much deeper than that. For one thing, the director, Rolands (Cambridge B.A., Duke University Ph. D.), was a strong union member and at the bottom of it all.

Because Rust felt he had to be in complete control of a multi-national university with several campuses kept uniform so that students could freely move from one to another, he sought to maintain autocratic control, and the faculty was in rebellion, with Rolands not only supporting them but egging them on.

The entire problem had to be sorted out within two weeks after Dunn's arrival, when the spring quarter was due to begin. The British Mediation Service was called in, and despite their doing an excellent job, it became clear that Rolands was the chief stumbling block to any solution.

Rust and Dunn spoke on the telephone several times, to keep Rust abreast of developments and for whatever instructions Rust may have wished to offer. Dunn was consistently told to use his own judgment and achieve the best results he could.

Using that judgment, Dunn offered Rolands one year's salary if he would cancel his contract and go off into the night, publicly giving whatever reason he chose. When that was refused, Bob offered him two year's salary, which he also turned down.

With no other alternative, Dunn called a meeting of all the students. Each time he tried to say something, he was hissed. Finally, when he told the students that they had heard nothing but the point of view of the faculty in their classes for weeks, but had never heard the other side, they quieted down and let him speak. He explained some of the problems and stated that in view of the intransigence of the director and faculty, school would not reopen for the spring quarter. He said further that the university would pay the transportation to San Diego for all students who wished to transfer to that campus.

The campus was closed and more than half of the students opted to transfer to San Diego. Pending the sale of the property, it was arranged that the chef and his assistant would remain on the premises to keep away any squatters. Since it was a long and expensive process to remove squatters legally, retaining and compensating the two men was both necessary and economical.

The firm of Knight, Frank and Rutley was engaged as land agents to sell the property, and after a short time Barclay's Bank was found to be a prospective buyer. The Bank offered far less than the asking price of $800,000 and Dr. Rust was inclined to accept the lower offer. The land agents insisted, however, that the university should stand fast at its asking price. They said that several of the bank's executives lived in the area, and that they were very anxious to obtain the property to use not only as an employee training facility but also as a sort of private club for themselves—and there was no other property available in the area.

Dr. Rust agreed to remain in England for several extremely anxious days, until the real estate firm's advice was revealed to be correct—the bank accepted the offer at the asking price!

There followed two other difficult obstacles to the final conclusion of the matter. The sale to Barclay's included a provision that there would be no one on the property at the time of transfer of possession. The chef and his assistant, discovering their strong bargaining position, alleged that they themselves were squatters and would not leave the premises unless legally evicted—a time-consuming process which would effectively block the sale.

Dunn worked out a loan of $5000 to each of them, evidenced by a note which would be uncollectible, and that problem was solved. After the sale, however, the London office on Ironmonger Lane of Peat, Marwick and Mitchell, the American accounting firm, advised that unless properly handled, the Inland Revenue might interpret the then new capital gains law to include the university's land sale.

Fortunately, Bob Dunn and a local solicitor were able to avoid any tax by showing that the university had ceased operations some months before, and thus was not a foreign corporation doing business in Britain, and hence any gain on the sale of the property was not taxable.

The last facility purchased by the university in England was a former Masonic School for Boys on the north side of London, where college operations were continued.

Contemporaneous with the efforts to establish a campus in Britain were the efforts to establish a college in Kenya, after Nairobi had been decided upon from the standpoints of accessibility, climate, need and viability. Dick Lareau described the early efforts at finding the proper facility and obtaining the proper authorizations for remodeling, construction and operation.

Apparently after numerous difficulties with the inevitable bureaucrats, Dick noticed a University of California (his own Alma Mater) diploma on the wall of the office of the Minister of Education, a ranking official in the all-black Kenyan government. Out of character, but determined to pull out every stop to achieve the university's objectives, Dick cheered "Go, Bears" the next time the Education Minister entered the room! Thereafter Lareau could do no wrong and negotiations for permits and authorizations proceeded without delay.

At its inception, the school in Kenya was at the college level, until it was learned that better high school training was needed in order to train a sufficient number of qualified students to support the college. So it was that high school programs were developed, then later a full K-12 program, and then as the years went by the students trained in the International University of Kenya lower schools became its college students. (It was discovered very early in President Rust's international efforts that the name *United States* International was both imposing and threatening in most countries.)

Despite the success of the Nairobi school, it was a financial drain at first because while money was permitted to be put in, no moneys were permitted to be taken out of Kenya. The result was that whatever cash flow was generated could only be used there or reinvested in that campus. On the other hand, it later ceased to be a drain on the finances of the university in San Diego, except for one enormous loss to be reported later in the odyssey.

The Nairobi campus has continued to operate and flourish, now with some 1600 students, primarily in college classes and with substantial interchange of students. Between Kenya and the United States at least, Dr. Rust's dream is in part being realized.

In Mexico City it was discovered that the University of the Americas was building a new and larger campus, making its excellent old one available. It was a natural for USIU, and Dr. Rust wasted little time in acquiring it. The school operated successfully for several years until the need to raise money to help handle the fiscal problems in San Diego made it necessary to try to sell that campus.

With no prospects in sight, a British architect, resident in Mexico City and with excellent government connections, approached Rust and Dunn. He said that he might be able to find a purchaser at a fair price, but he would require a commission of 15%. Although the commission sounded unconscionable, they felt that the price might be so adjusted as to make such a high commission palatable. And indeed, before long it was revealed that the Mexican government was the prospective purchaser of the property.

After the deal had been worked out, the price having been boosted enough to cover the commission, a meeting was held in the impressive offices of one of Mexico City's largest law firms. After several of the partners, in derby hats and with black umbrellas under their arms, had arrived for the meeting, there began an extended discussion of the place and manner of payment of the commission.

The request was first made that the payment be made in cash in Tijuana, to which Dunn demurred. Then it was suggested that it could be made in a bank in Barbados—whereupon Dunn said that the university was continuing to operate in Mexico at the sufferance of the Mexican government, and could not participate in any evasion of taxes. Dunn then said that if the law firm partners would sign a letter indicating that they would personally indemnify the university for any taxes or problems arising from the non-payment of the tax on the amount of the sales commission, the university would cooperate with them.

Ultimately, when the partners indicated their obvious unwillingness to provide any such indemnification, the Britisher reluctantly indicated he would pay the tax on the 15% commission—which undoubtedly meant considerable out-of-pocket cost to him on any portion of that commission which he must have had to share with others!

Thereafter the university moved to rented quarters in Mexico City, and that campus has remained in continuous operation, normally with an enrollment of one hundred to one hundred twenty students.

After Dr. Rust had zeroed in on Evian, on the shore of Lake Geneva, as the ideal location for a campus in France, it fell to Dick Lareau to help find the most desirable facility. There were three old hotels for sale, all three beautifully situated overlooking the lake on the hillside above the city, all three in deplorable condition. Rust chose the one which was the least expensive and which he thought could be most readily rehabilitated at reasonable cost. After it was purchased, all of the efforts to remodel, furnish, staff , and operate were begun, and for a few years it provided a happy experience to some French students and a small number of transfers from the San Diego campus.

(On Sabbatical leave in 1977, we visited Evian. While the location, the surroundings and the view were incomparable, we were disappointed in the condition of the once beautiful building which was that college campus. It was by then obviously suffering from the university's dire financial straits.)

There had at one time been consideration of Hong Kong and Taipei for the establishment of campuses, but instead Dr. Rust was able to enter into agreements for "sister" campuses in both those cities.

The desired Far Eastern campus was actually created in Japan, in the city of Kishiwada, some fifty miles south of Tokyo and across the bay from Osaka, Japan's second largest city. In its quest for a second airport to serve Tokyo, the Japanese government had built an enormous landfill in the bay at Kishiwada City. The newly-created land was to provide not only space for a new airport, but also a grand new development, including residential, educational and commercial facilites—and Dr. Rust was able to negotiate participation by USIU as one of the new educational entities.

Pending the completion of the infrastructure and the construction at Kishiwada, however, Rust discovered the availability of temporary two-storey pre-fabricated buildings, and the school was established in them, along with some rented classrooms in Tokyo. The school was operated in those facilities for several years, before it had to be closed because of the financial problems in San Diego. The great dream at Kishiwada, like so many other of Dr. Rust's dreams, was never fulfilled.

In addition to the foreign campuses, Dr. Rust also sought to establish two other American campuses, one on Maui in Hawaii, the other in Steamboat Springs, Colorado. Neither operated for any length of time, but in both instances, as with several of the transactions in foreign countries, the real estate purchases themselves (although there were often extensive operating losses), ultimately resulted in profits on the sale of the realty itself.

The sale of the Maui campus, also made when the university was *in extremis*, was to a government entity as the Mexican campus had been. Happily situated in an area surrounded by properties of the original old missionary families, the campus provided "Elmer, the mayor of Maui" an opportunity to establish a public facility as a thorn in their midst!

Bob Dunn recalled sitting in Elmer's magnificent offices with their 360 degree view, when he called the governor to say "I want some money", and after explaining why he needed it, it was apparently made available to Maui, and the sale was consummated.

(In 1975, when I was legal advisor to Bill Rust during Bob Dunn's absence in Kenya, the sale of the Steamboat Springs campus was just being concluded.)

Dr. Rust's grand visions, his hopes for an international alliance of colleges, were actually accomplished far beyond the imagination or expectations of his critics, and the Mexico City and Nairobi campuses at least have survived. That the grand plan of several more campuses was never fulfilled as he had hoped may have resulted from his short-comings, from failures of his associates, mistakes in business judgment, or any number of other reasons. That his intentions were laudable and his ideas sound, even that his dreams were valuable cannot be doubted—for all his faults as a fiscal manager (for which unfortunately he is primarily remembered) he exhibited throughout a dedication to strong moral principles, sound educational policies, and a desire for international peace and understanding.

Rust must be given credit first of all for the revival of the dormant law school. In addition, there can be no question that his dedication and purpose, his fund-raising efforts on the law school's behalf, and his insistence on high educational and moral standards were predominant in the molding of the school. But at the same time it must be said that his efforts at international expansion had an enormous impact on the law school. Particularly in the early 1970's, the great costs of those international adventures in dollars and their demands on his time, attention and concern, resulted in the law school's complete change of course.

LAW STUDENTS' CODE OF ETHICS

ALL STUDENTS OF THE LAW SCHOOL ARE PRESUMED TO BE
PERSONS OF HONOR. GOOD CHARACTER. AND UNQUESTIONABLE
INTEGRITY. ACCORDINGLY. EACH IS ALWAYS EXPECTED TO
CONDUCT HIMSELF IN A MANNER THAT WILL REFLECT
FAVORABLY UPON THE SCHOOL AND THE LEGAL PROFESSION.

How simple and direct it was!

Dick Lareau, university architect and tennis player extraordinaire

The law school reopened in most modest downtown quarters.

Bill Potter, with co-editor John Ramsey, hands early Law Review to Dr. Rust—Professor Meiners and Dean Castetter look on

The new law school building on the Point Loma campus

Law Library

Students in the courtyard

The view was better than the collection

Professor Burby teaches a summer class

The first moot court room

*Student wives:
Petti-Court*

Commencement exercises in the former Theosophical Institute's Greek Theatre

Pipe Dream—the proposed new law school building on the Elliott campus

Justice William O. Douglas visits with the author on Point Loma.

Dean and Marj Castetter with Toni and the brand new professor dining in Tijuana

Cal Western's first national championship

Prof. George N. Gafford of La Jolla, left, and student John Casey of Del Mar, center, help display the national championship trophy won by the California Western University School of Law in competition last month in Los Angeles. Other team members are Frank Baker, second from left, and Robert Fredrick, second from right. At right is Law School dean Robert K. Castetter.

The Second Floor

In the lounge an atmosphere of an exclusive club has been attained through the skilful use of great, high windows, richly draped, impressive columns, a gorgeously decorated ceiling, and the most comfortable of furnishings. Every nook and corner of the lounge suggests inviting comfort where club members may find a retreat in which to enjoy the companionship of their friends.

Casement windows give access to a roomy, tiled terrace with an ever interesting view. The huge fireplace will be a popular gathering place, with the warmth of its great logs sending good cheer and comradeship into every corner of the lounge. The beauty and comfort of the furnishings will provide rest and inspiration to our members.

The Dining Room

Through a high, vaulted passage leading from the lounge you enter the dining room. It is divided into a main dining room and two separate, smaller sections by means of massive columns supporting an enriched concrete ceiling fifteen feet above the floor. The Ladies' dining room can be closed off when desired, or opened into the main room, providing a seating capacity of four hundred guests.

At one end is the convenient buffet counter providing a quick and comfortable service.

A very modern kitchen occupies the North wall of the building.

From the ladies' dining room a door leads to the attractive terrace. The beauty of the appointments and excellence of the cuisine will make this a popular meeting place for members, their friends and their ladies.

The Billiard Room

Balancing the dining room on the Third street side are the Billiard and Card rooms, occupying a space 92 by 58 feet, with a 15 foot ceiling. Players will enjoy the beauty of the surroundings. Here, again, massive columns combine with attractive draperies and a decorated ceiling to give an atmosphere of the exclusive club. The billiard section holds ten tables, insuring ample accommodations. There are long, upholstered benches on two sides. Large windows give access to a large, wrought iron railed balcony.

The Card Room

The Card room is spacious and well ventilated. On this side of the room are also the Secretary's office, Board room and a cigar counter.

Everything possible has been done to provide comfortable and pleasant surroundings so that club members will get the full benefit of the recreational features of the new home.

The Elk's building was to be like an exclusive men's club.

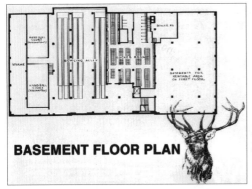

With gymnasium and reading room

THIRD FLOOR PLAN

BASEMENT FLOOR PLAN

Bowling alley, hand ball courts and locker room

Discouragingly open empty spaces

Bronze door plates and doorknobs reminiscent of the building's Elk ancestry

Majestic and imposing

But stark and sparsely furnished

Mirrors and barres were great for dancing but not to teach law.

Law students pitched in.

Commencement in Balboa Park for the newly-independent school

Chapter VII

From Point Loma to Cedar Street

Although becoming a full-time law teacher after more than twenty-five years as a practicing attorney was very different, it was not at all difficult for me—nor for the law students—to become acclimated to life in Southern California. We determined to spend our first Christmas in Baja California.

Only the most intrepid of adventurers, in four-wheel drive vehicles, then ventured south of Ensenada since there were almost no roads from there to La Paz. So we drove on the mainland of Mexico past Hermosillo and Ciudad Obregon to Topolobampo. There we put the car on a newly-established ferry to La Paz and then drove the one hundred or so miles to Cabo San Lucas.

When we drove up to the entrance to *Las Tres Palmillas* in our dusty three-year-old sedan with its California license plates, two men rushed up to us to open the doors.

"*Señor*, we cannot believe it!"

"What?"

"Do you mean to say you drove here in *that* car—through the BAJA?"

Realizing that they apparently were not aware of the ferry from Topolobampo to La Paz, I smiled and said "*Si, si. De San Diego. ¿Porque no?*" (Yes, from San Diego. Why not?)

They walked around the car, looking at us in rapt admiration. Only the next day did we admit the truth, much to their laughter and embarrassment.

During the following short spring vacation break we drove from the La Jolla seashore to Palm Springs in the desert and then up to a little cabin in the snow in the nearby Laguna mountains. How could a law school in such a location not be a magnet to students and faculty alike?

But as wonderful as was the area with all its distractions, I was anxious and fascinated with my new career as a law professor. At first it still seemed that I was on leave from the law practice, almost as if I were on vacation from its pressures and responsibilities! After so many years of part-time teaching, I was completely comfortable with appearing before classes and lecturing or questioning or responding to questions.

But soon the difference became apparent between being a full-time teacher and teaching part-time—when my chief concerns and obligations had continued to be to my clients. Now the students were my chief obligation and the law school was my career. And as each day passed, as conscious as I had always been of the importance of teachers' attitudes, I became more aware of how great an influence a law teacher can have who is with the students on a daily basis. Of particular interest to me were the reports I heard from students about certain impressions about attorneys and the practice of law they had gained from some members of the faculty. There seemed to be a disdain for practicing lawyers and their morals, their agendas and their abilities.

There was an aura of distrust of attorneys which to me seemed diametrically opposed to the attitude which I thought should prevail and be taught in a law school. One or two of the faculty were actually scornful of the Philistines, the money-seekers, the practitioners of the very discipline which they were teaching! I had heard it said that students entered law school with the highest of ideals and left law school disillusioned and bereft of those ideals. I determined that it would be my mission to encourage and support the ideals of my students. It would be my goal to help them become part of the vast majority of practicing lawyers who were doing their best honestly and diligently to sustain the rule of law, to serve the best interests of their clients, their community and their nation.

Before long I detected that many students were becoming aware of my references to good results that lawyers had obtained and the actual steps which had been taken to accomplish them. Perhaps too often I caught myself using examples from my own practice to explain and demonstrate various solutions. The more that students seemed to ask me questions about actual practice and the more I worried about the impression students received about the law as it is applied in practice, the more a basic dichotomy became my concern.

Should law school be a graduate school in the discipline of law or should it be a professional school training students to be practicing attorneys? The question has been often addressed in one form or another, and over the last sixty years I have seen the answer swinging back and forth and in between. In the nineteen thirties law students were required to learn the forms of pleadings (with Latin names) used in old English common law but even then no longer used anywhere in the United States. They read cases from the English Assizes in the fourteenth and fifteenth centuries (sometimes even earlier!), cases involving negotiable instruments developed by the ancient Law Merchant, and learned many time-honored legal maxims. These were only a few of the elements in the erudition which it was believed members of the legal profession should gain in law school.

Never was any thought given to teaching students how actually to write a contract, draw and file a pleading, prepare a journal entry, form a corporation or draft a real property or chattel mortgage. No schools had clinics, and certainly the trial of a lawsuit was not something to be taught in school. One of my professors, when asked why, told me: "The trial of a lawsuit is a pedestrian talent you will learn after you leave school." But in later years, as many law schools discarded most esoteric courses and had fewer and fewer required courses, they began operating legal clinics, and many offered more and more courses considered "practical."

It fascinated me to hear faculty discussions of these matters, both by my colleagues and at conferences or meetings with other faculties. There seemed to be, as has been my complaint in most areas of life, extreme views on both sides. There were those academics and purists who insisted that students should be taught to think as lawyers (I never really knew exactly what that meant), and that legal scholarship and reasoning, exposure to the great appellate legal decisions and learned commentaries was the sole job of the law school. Opposed to them were those (far fewer) who believed law schools were really trade schools whose job was merely to teach students how to obtain and serve clients, how to bill them and make a living practicing law.

The fundamental problem with too much emphasis on the practical, on the "real world" evolved in my mind from my own experience. During the first few years of my new career I felt very confident in showing the students "how it's done", and I was flattered to have them come to me to tell them "what it's really like". But as the years went by I grew less confident, concerned that perhaps some of what I was telling them had changed. Then it was that I became fully aware of the problem with too much practicality. Although I had often heard the complaint from laymen that "kids coming out of law school don't even know how to find the courthouse"—might not the courthouse have been moved right after they graduated?

But sound legal principles and legal reasoning are not moved or replaced, and the common law changes very slowly. From these thoughts came my realization that there must be a most careful mix, difficult to achieve, of educating cultured professionals who understand the law but who are also practitioners competent to advise and proficiently serve and represent their clients.

With this realization came the determination in my new career to do all that I could to fulfill that dual role of the law school: to encourage students to become informed, cultured and articulate citizens and true scholars of the law as well as able and ethical practitioners skilled in their profession.

California Western School of Law of United States International University, despite its overly-long and pretentious name, was a homey little school in 1969, perched as it was almost alone on the top of the cliff overlooking the beautiful Pacific. It had a dean, the dean's secretary, an admissions secretary and one office secretary. The librarian was an assistant professor, aided by a staff of one, overseeing a library allegedly containing thirty-five thousand volumes, and there was a full-time faculty of four professors, two associate professors, and an assistant professor. The bulletin designated me as a visiting associate professor.

The total student body grew very slowly and gradually during the school's first ten years, from eight students in 1958, to some one hundred and sixty in 1967. There were quantum leaps however in 1968, with one hundred and one entering first year students, and in 1969, when the first year class alone numbered one hundred and twenty. Along with the school's growing reputation there was little doubt that the popularity of the fictional Perry Mason on television and the growing enthusiasm for new legal horizons among the young contributed to the great increase in law school enrollment throughout the country.

In 1970, the entering class was one hundred ninety four, and in the following three years the school grew to a student body of over four hundred and fifty.

But as long as it remained on Point Loma, the keynote of the school seemed to be informality—I don't believe the expression "laid back" had yet been used, but it would certainly have applied. This is not to say that there were not excellent instruction and conscientious study, and both faculty and students dedicated to their missions. Although the dress grew gradually less formal, the faculty were all addressed as "professor", and in most classes the students were addressed by their last names.

There was an active Student Bar Association, a scholarly and carefully edited Law Review, and an equally erudite International Law Journal (one of very few among American law schools). There was a

Moot Court Board from which were chosen the interschool appellate moot court competition teams, an International Law Society, a student magazine called *La Balanza*, two legal fraternities, and the Petti-Court.

In 1972, I established the Law Office Competition Board. By 1973, the name of the Petti-Court was changed to Cal-Western Law Wives (and later to Le Gals!), I changed the name of the Law Office Competition Board to the Client Counseling Board, and the staid *La Balanza* became a strident student newspaper called the *Commentary*.

Also during my first four years, several new faculty members were added: Murray Galinson, a former assistant U.S. Attorney and private practitioner; Lawrence Lee, who had taught at Southern Methodist University and the University of Pittsburgh; Lowell Miller, former member of the Committee of Bar Examiners and successful practitioner; George Stevens, a former dean of the law schools of the Universities of Buffalo, Washington, and Lewis and Clark, and a professor at several law schools including Case Western Reserve, my law school alma mater and where I had also taught; and Robert Weninger, a C.P.A., former public defender and practitioner. In addition, the cadre of adjunct lecturers, all members of the local bench and bar, was substantially enlarged.

The interesting feature of these many additions to the faculty, as well as promotions and granting of tenure within the faculty, was that they were made by Dean Castetter and President Rust, without any faculty participation. The principle of faculty governance, so treasured in most schools, did not exist. When my status was changed from "visiting," and then the next year from associate professor to professor, and within the next year or two when I was granted tenure, the other faculty members had no voice—nor did I in any changes in their status or the appointment of new faculty. We were told that promotions and tenure were approved by the University Senate, but as far as we knew, that body merely provided a rubber stamp to the wishes of the president.

Nevertheless, there were advantages to what was truly a very loose and informal benevolent dictatorship. We were all free to go our own way and pursue our own interests without interference, there were no conflicts or cliques or jealousies among the faculty, and we seemed a cohesive, happy family.

The dean was genial, gregarious and completely unsophisticated. Somewhat portly and pompous, he was nevertheless much liked by the students for his folksiness and his recurrent slogans or mottos, which he used and repeated at every opportunity. He had such favorites as "Every day is a good day, but some days are even better than others," "Keep striving," "Peace is the motto for the day," and "There is not enough justice to go around."

Although the faculty parking lot was cut out of the cliff a short walk below the law school, there was room for one or two cars right next to the school. There it was that Marj Castetter, the dean's wife, would park their car on many an afternoon. Students would stop and talk with her as she waited until the dean, usually in a black sport shirt and a bolo tie, was ready to go home.

Despite the existence of an Admissions Committee of the faculty which passed on admissions, there too an air of informality and benevolence obtained. The dean retained substantial license to admit students. His judgment was good, and many were admitted whose credentials would normally have denied them. And many among those have become successful and have been forever grateful to him.

One of the dean's favorite projects was the Mexican Law Program which he established in an effort to advance mutual trust and respect between Mexico and the United States. Begun in 1966, the program involved inviting Mexican lawyers, law teachers and government officials to speak at the law school. Students attended the symposia without academic credit, and for several years the program provided interesting speakers for the school, numerous visits to Mexico for the dean and his wife, and considerable social activity. Although the Law Review published an excellent symposium on Mexican law, student interest eventually waned and the program ended in the early eighties.

As is true in all schools, many decisions had to be made by the faculty and the dean with respect to the dismissal or retention of students, and there again the dean exercised his poetic license. Among the most difficult tasks I had to perform was talking to a student who had to be told that dismissal was inevitable. The kindest and most effective explanation I would give was that everyone has different aptitudes, and that apparently that student's was not the study of law but was undoubtedly some other endeavor.

Coming to law school highly recommended by a professor and the dean of students of the University of San Diego, that is what one student was written at the end of his first year in law at California Western. The dean suggested that perhaps he may want to enter a graduate school of business or investments and "we would be pleased to help you in that regard." Dominelli apparently adopted the suggestion and later established a very large and high profile securities business allegedly dealing in foreign currency arbitrage with claimed exorbitant profits.[24]

With turmoil and agitation rampant on many a university campus in the early 1970's, the USIU campuses, and certainly the law school, were free of any such problems. What did happen at California Western, however, was a proliferation of student concerns and organizations. They formed women student groups, Latin students, Asian students, environmental groups, criminal defense advocates, poverty law groups, and a legal clinic—until soon we could not provide spaces in which they could meet for even an hour at a time!

Although there was a university bookstore which had formerly sold books and supplies for the law school, when problems arose with that store, the Student Bar Association instead was provided a small space under the stairway to the Moot Court to operate a bookstore, and allowed to retain the profits for its own purposes.

---

[24] J. David Dominelli's J. David and Co. mulcted investors of millions of dollars, and he was ultimately convicted of one of the largest securities frauds in San Diego history.

At the beginning of each school session, tables were set up in the central courtyard next to the stairway, where the new and used books were stacked, and the students crowded around to make their purchases. Throughout the year that courtyard provided an area where all paths crossed for both students and faculty, and helped create a remarkable camaraderie.

There was about the school and the cozy little building, with its incredible vista, a certain charm and refreshing naivete which made it a sunny island of peace in troubled times. Before the storm clouds of the university's cash-flow problems darkened the mood of the faculty and the students, all was peace and tranquillity.

The students played touch football, with some faculty participation, and some of us grew to know the students better on the university tennis courts. There was an annual black-tie school dinner dance, and an annual "Law Revue" was inaugurated in which enthusiastic students with varying degrees of musical and terpsichorean talent gently lampooned the faculty.

Each spring there was a cheerful luncheon at which the new Law Review and International Law Journal editorial boards were announced and the faculty rewarded students for outstanding achievements. Those luncheons, however, grew to unmanageable proportions when the Student Bar Association was permitted to make its increasingly ribald awards—until one student, submitting to the then current fad of "streaking," ran nude across the dining room in front of the speakers' table!

In great contrast to the daily informalities of the school, the commencement exercises were formal and impressive. Held in the beautiful outdoor Greek Theater of by-gone Theosophical Society times, graduation was both conventional and festive. Dr. Rust led the colorful academic procession and presided over the ceremonies. There was inspiring music provided by the university orchestra, and even the typical commencement speakers sounded wiser and less trite among the swaying trees in the bright sunshine.

The University Bulletin for both 1971-1972 and 1972-1973 stated that the university had several campuses: three in San Diego (the original California Western Campus on Point Loma, the downtown Center for the Performing Arts, and the Elliott Campus), one in Steamboat Springs, Colorado, one in England, one in Kenya, one in Mexico, and one in Hawaii. It said that U.S. International University in England was the first of a number of projected "university centers abroad," and the second was Nairobi International School, a secondary school preparing students from Africa for admission to the University. It was further stated that a university-level program in Kenya was projected for 1971 and that *Universidad Internacional de Mexico*, the third "university center abroad", opened in the fall of 1970 in Mexico City.

Both those bulletins also noted that a law school physical plant for a student body of 450 was to be constructed at the university's Elliott campus north of San Diego, and that the "Office of the Dean of the School of Law will give adequate notice of the actual date of the move so that law students can make appropriate living arrangements."

While there were some indications that all was not well for the university financially, all faculty salaries were still honored on time, and as far as we knew, all bills were being paid. The library budget however was much smaller than we would have preferred, faculty salaries were lower than at comparable law schools, and there was a tight rein on all travel and other expenditures. Nevertheless none of us saw any need for real alarm. On the contrary, as much as we loved the Point Loma campus, students and faculty alike felt an optimism about the promised new and larger law school facility.

In 1971, Louis Brown, a Los Angeles practicing attorney and a professor at the University of Southern California law school wanted to establish a new interschool competition named in honor of his father. His thought was to provide an incentive for greater interest and study of preventive law and of office advice to clients rather than on the then (and in my opinion even now) major emphasis on appellate court litigation. He met with me in San Diego and invited me to Los

Angeles in planning the Emil Brown Mock Law Office Competition. The "Mock Law Office" bothered me (and probably others) and was later changed to "Client Counseling," which was the name I had given our student organization.

The format which finally evolved for the competition was for there to be teams of two lawyers each who had received a letter from a client generally describing his problem, which the competing teams were provided in advance of the competition. In that way they knew the general area of law involved and were able to do some preliminary research in anticipation of the client's possible concerns.

Then in the actual competition, in the presence of the judges, the client chosen and briefed by the host school entered the lawyers' office for the interview. It was up to the student-lawyers to engender confidence, elicit enough information to be able to give proper advice, make appropriate fee arrangements, and explain future action if necessary. Everything was to be as practical and realistic as possible.

The first competition attracted only a very few schools, but I was determined that ours would be among them. Managing to recruit several interested students, we held an intraschool competition and fielded the winning team of David Freeman and Maurice Evans, with Bob Mulcahy as alternate. Evans had been out in the world for some years before he came to law school and from his performance I realized that talking with a client and giving credible advice required greater maturity and life experience than the preparation of an appellate brief and the argument to a court. The Freeman-Evans team were national runners-up.

In the following year, with the previous year's success, there was greater interest among the students and the winners of the intraschool competition were two older students, John Casey, who had been a Lt. Colonel in the Air Force and Bob Fredrick, who had had a successful career as a real estate developer. They, along with Frank Baker as a third member, were very able and unusually conscientious, and we worked hard together (often at our home in the evenings and on week-ends)—resulting in their winning first the regional and then the national championship in a greatly expanded competition. The finals were held in Los Angeles before a panel of distinguished judges, one of whom was Frank Wells, later the president of the Walt Disney Company until his death in a helicopter crash in 1994.

The school's international law competition teams under the tutelage of Professor Lay also fared remarkably well in competitions, placing second and third in the nationwide Philip Jessup International Moot Court Competition, winning best memorial and best oralist (Tim Smith) in the United States, and winning best memorial in the California International Moot Court competition, as well as several regional team titles. The school's outstanding success in these international competitions, along with its international law journal, the Mexican Law program and the proximity to Mexico, helped establish a modest reputation throughout the country in the field of international law.

The Casey-Fredrick client counseling team was succeeded by a team of Laurie Laws, Howard Harris and Shelly O'Neil. Again we worked long and hard, and they too won the national championship at Notre Dame law school. Ours was the only law school to have won two national Client Counseling titles. Barnabas Sears and Lyman Tondel, former Illinois and New Jersey Bar presidents, and Judiciary Committee counsel Albert Jenner were the judges.

Sam Chapin, with his wide court experience as a labor lawyer in New York had been an adjunct member of the faculty, teaching trial practice and coaching the appellate moot court teams since 1965. He gave up teaching shortly after I joined the faculty, whereupon I took over his responsibilities. He had already experimented some, and provided valuable precedents for me in the relatively novel area of trial practice instruction to law students. Greatly implementing and improving the original format for student jury trials created by General Snedeker, he provided for me an excellent foundation upon which to build and embellish the still infant discipline.

Late in 1972, with the hopes and plans for a beautiful new law school building on the Elliott campus of USIU a distant dream, President Rust informed Dean Castetter that the law school was to be moved into the building in downtown San Diego occupied by the university's School for Performing Arts. There was even the suggestion that some of the building would be shared with the SPA.

One Sunday afternoon, before Toni and I were to have dinner with the Castetters, as we then did on many occasions, they suggested we stop to look at the "terrible" building on Cedar Street. They were both devastated by the prospect and extremely critical of "Bully Bill," as the dean called Rust, for causing the move.

"Can you imagine leaving our beautiful campus for this?" asked Marj. "It's filthy dirty, it's depressing—it's just awful."

The dean reassured her: "Now, Marj, it's not that bad—absolutely horrible is what it is, and I guess it is depressing."

Toni and I had an entirely different reaction. We were fascinated by the beauty of the stately Italian Renaissance building, the towering lobby entrance, the arches and pediments, and the rhythmic windows. To us it had instant tradition, the stability of a real law school building: solid, spacious, and impressive, with its grand central staircase, its fluted columns and colorfully painted ceilings.

"Really, Marj," said Toni, "with a lot of hard work cleaning and sprucing it up, getting rid of some of the black paint and black curtains, this building will be wonderful.

"Do you know, I actually have wonderful memories of attending De Molay[25] dances in this building when I was at San Diego High. They were held in that beautiful big room in front on the second floor."

"Well, George, if you really think it's so great, as dean I hereby appoint you to the faculty committee to work out the plans to make this bad dream into a law school building."

---

[25] A fraternal organization open to young men between their 15th and 25th birthdays, memorializing Jacques De Molay, the last grand master of the Knights Templar.

And in December of 1972, began the enormous task of planning and accomplishing the remodeling and furnishing of that 83,000 square foot building into a suitable law school facility within an incredibly limited budget or no budget at all.

Now registered as a City of San Diego Historical Site, the four-storey building at 350 Cedar Street was designed by Quayle Brothers architects and built by the Morley Golden construction company in 1929-1930 for the Benevolent and Fraternal Order of Elks #168. Still remaining in the building are many of the original bronze doorknobs bearing the beautifully cast head and antlers of a magnificent elk.

The Elks were an outgrowth of members of the theatrical and musical association known as the "Jolly Corks" in New York City in the early winter of 1867-68. The name was officially changed because the elk is "fleet of foot, timorous of wrong but ever ready to combat in defense of self or the female of the species." They felt the elk displayed admirable qualities that members of the fraternity should emulate. Their charitable contributions included the care of their members in sickness and death, raising money for handicapped children, hearing and vision screening, and for the training of cerebral palsy children. The organization emphasized a strong moral commitment and devotion to country, and was the first national fraternal organization to require each of its subordinate lodges to celebrate Flag Day with appropriate observances.

In building the Elks Hall on Cedar Street, the San Diego lodge unfortunately over-extended its financial capability. This, combined with the depression years and declining membership led to the insolvency of the lodge, resulting in the property being taken over by the Pacific Mutual Life Insurance Company in 1938.

Between 1938 and 1941, the building was rented to the Department of Motor Vehicles and was used as their administrative headquarters. In 1939, it had been considered for purchase by the San Diego Board of Education, but in 1941 Pacific Mutual sold the building to the Masonic Temple Association.

The San Diego Lodge No. 35 Free and Accepted Masons was the first Masonic Lodge established in Southern California, a member of the order of free masonry which originated in the middle ages when the great cathedrals were being built. Masonic guilds originally formed to protect the integrity and excellence of their craft, the lodges were opened to "speculative" members who were "non-operative" Masons in the 17th century. The square, plumb bob and level became the figurative guides for the building of careers and great societies, and the ritual of the order became paramount as the tie to the ancient masonic tradition.

The symbols of that Masonic ritual were still evident and omnipresent in the former Elks Hall and then the Masonic Temple, when the law school was making plans to move into the building in 1973.

In 1967, the Masonic lodge, primarily because of the problem of parking in downtown San Diego, moved to a new home in Mission Valley, and the Masonic Temple was sold to California Western University of San Diego, later renamed USIU. It then became the home of the School for Performing Arts, as well as being often used by the San Diego Symphony for recitals and practice.

In the spring of 1973, amidst all of the planning for the move downtown, the Student Bar Association, with funds earned from the operation of the bookstore, was able to invite Justice Stanley Mosk of the California Supreme Court to speak with the students. Among their most significant achievements for the school was to host a three-day visit by Supreme Court Justice William O. Douglas, a great favorite with all the students and many of the faculty. It was my privilege to chat alone with him to reminisce about the time when he had been the Chairman of the Securities and Exchange Commission and I had been one of its fledgling attorneys.

And it was in early 1973 also that the financial problems of the university were becoming more and more evident, explaining the decision to move the law school to Cedar Street, and culminating in the sale of the beautiful Point Loma campus. It had always appeared to me and no doubt to the university Board of Trustees as well, that almost any debt within reason could always be satisfied by the sale of a portion of the incredibly valuable ocean-front land of the Point Loma campus. However, the city refused to alter the zoning or the conditional use permit under which the land was being used. That conditional use permit limited the educational use of the entire piece of land to 3000 students. At one point the City Planning Department actually urged that the land be placed in a holding zone of Agricultural-ten acre minimum! Profitable subdivision or partial sale was severely restricted, and even educational use extremely limited.

It was a fortuitous coincidence that a professor at seventy-year-old Nazarene College, which had outgrown its campus in Pasadena, California, learned of the availability of the Point Loma property while on a visit to San Diego. He promptly reported that fact to the Nazarene administration, which was not concerned with the student limitation, and the very difficult negotiations were begun. Badly in need of the sale proceeds to satisfy creditors, USIU had to transfer the liens on the Point Loma property and refinance the Elliott campus in complicated transactions with severe time constraints and innumerable problems. Days or even hours before the contemplated closing, the immediate requirement for $125,000 in cash from USIU was disclosed.

In desperation and with nowhere else to turn, Bill Rust telephoned a neighbor to a piece of property he had inherited from his family in northern California. Although it was extremely valuable land and worth a great deal more, Rust told the neighbor that he would sell it to him for $125,000, if that amount was paid immediately in cash. The neighbor grasped the opportunity, the cash was made available, and the sale to Nazarene College was consummated.

So it was that the law school's promised new building on the Elliott campus was a forgotten dream, and the law school was instead to be moved to the building on Cedar Street in downtown San Diego.

The architects, the members of the faculty committee and I were charged with the challenge of converting an Elks Hall, then a Masonic Temple, and then a School for Performing Arts into a law school facility. We faced a daunting but fascinating task—and we were a congenial group. Lareau, the architect, was extremely knowledgeable, George Stevens had been several times a law school dean, Murray Galinson had been a practicing lawyer and capable business man, and Houston Lay, a very practical-minded man, had been a diplomat, writer and teacher.

When the law school's new home was the Elks Hall, there were six regulation bowling alleys and two handball courts in the basement. After extensive remodeling of the basement by the Masons, the School for Performing Arts removed the bowling alleys, installed several sound-proof instrumental practice rooms, a Children's Theater, dining room and a kitchen.

On the first floor the Elks had provided the grand entrance, a barber shop, several retail stores and other rentable areas. The Masons and the SPA had retained the large entrance area, but the SPA had painted all the walnut-paneled wainscoting black! In the rest of the main floor they had erected partitions creating large open areas and several individual offices, including a paneled suite, used for a time by Dr. Rust as his downtown headquarters.

Above the main floor there was a partial balcony accessible part-way up the handsome central staircase. Little use seemed to have been made of it by any of the former occupants. There was a landing at the head of the staircase, with an arched window. From there double stairs led to the second floor, and then open double stairs to the third floor, with a huge arched window at the landing between the second and third floors.

On the second floor the Elks had had a lounge hall, the main dining room, a ladies' dining room, kitchen, billiard room and card room. The Masons had created two large ballrooms on that floor, while the SPA had built several classrooms and converted those ballrooms into great dance studios with flexible hardwood flooring and barres and mirrors on all the walls.

The Elks had installed a gymnasium and regulation-size basketball court on the third floor with a balcony on three sides, and with a kitchenette. In the center of that floor, at the head of the stairs were a lounge hall and a reading room with a huge fireplace and a vaulted ceiling, handsomely painted. The Lodge Room was on the other side of the building, with 500 permanent seats and a total seating capacity of 1000, plus a small balcony seating 86. The Lodge Room was 93 feet by 58 feet, with a 24-foot ceiling and provision for the installation of a pipe organ.

The Masons had retained the gymnasium and its balcony. They had, however, removed the seating and remodeled the Lodge Room into their Ceremonial Room, replete with lovely wall lamps, a lighted Masonic leaded glass window, and a huge chandelier in the room's center, bearing the Masonic emblem—and had installed the pipes for an organ.

The SPA converted the gymnasium into a 300-seat theater, with a proscenium arch, curtains, complete stage equipment and lighting. In the Masons' Ceremonial Room they had erected a stage and temporary seating stands, painted the walls black, and had black curtains supported by movable posts dividing and covering most of the incredible beauty of the mahogany-paneled room with its magnificent painted, vaulted ceiling.

There was a very old stove which had apparently been used by the Elks and the Masons in a small kitchen on the fourth floor, but the SPA had used the entire floor for the storage, cleaning, ironing and repair of costumes. There were long racks and dozens of wires and outlets for irons, washing machines and lamps. Large shower rooms and lavatories were dirty and apparently unused. The utter disregard in which the entire beautiful building had been held by the SPA was difficult to believe—but the fourth floor was the most disreputable-looking area of all.

Our committee spent hours and hours over a period of more than six months walking through the beautiful building which had been so desecrated by the SPA, studying the plans which were available, and trying to determine how the space could best be transformed into a law school facility at the least possible expense.

We spent a great deal of time with Dick Lareau as university architect, as well as Hermann Zillgens, his young assistant recently come from Germany. They made many studies and drew several preliminary plans. We asked other faculty members for suggestions, considered the configurations of other law schools, made and discarded many ideas and many plans. We first reached agreement on the principal use of the basement and each of the other four floors, and then had to delineate the particular plans for each.

On January 10, 1973, our committee presented a twelve-page memorandum to the dean and faculty setting forth specific recommendations for the law school's new home, and on January 24, thirteen pages of revised proposals were submitted, which included furniture and equipment needs, and such details as drinking fountains and locked faculty mail boxes. On March 6, the dean sent a memo to the faculty and the next day to Dick Lareau saying that the working drawings for the building revisions as outlined by the faculty building committee had received the "go ahead" signal from Dr. Rust, and that the library stacks would be ordered in time for August 1 delivery, so that classes could begin as scheduled by the end of August.

The lower floor, as the basement was to be named, would be devoted to library, with the sound-proof practice rooms to be made into individual and group study rooms.

Most of the main floor was to be library, with the administrative offices and many of the faculty offices off a hallway around the perimeter, and the law review and international law journal using the rest of the space.

There were to be faculty secretaries and some faculty offices on the mezzanine. On the second floor would be three tiered classrooms, one smaller classroom and a seminar room, a model attorney's office with one-way glass for observation, student aid office and student lockers. There was also space allocated for a legal clinic.

The theater on the third floor was to be retained as an auditorium, while the handsome former Elks' and Masons' reading room was to be the Faculty-Student Reading Room. A bookstore was to be built next to the auditorium, and the Masons' Ceremonial Room was to become the moot court.

The fourth floor was to house the student lunch room and lounge, showers, recreation room and student activity rooms.

Upon being told of the "go ahead," everyone naively expected the recommendations and the architects' plans would be carried out. Looked forward to with anticipation were an orderly move into a large and beautiful building, handsomely remodeled efficient and spacious classrooms, a well-appointed library, attractive administrative and faculty offices, a magnificent moot court, and ample comfortable space for all student activities.

Dreamers that we were, we expected very soon to have three amphitheater-type classrooms with permanent swivel-chair seating, hard-wired amplification systems, and podiums. There would be new clocks, bulletin boards and blackboards, electrical outlets for electric typewriters, special attention to acoustics, lighting, heating, air-conditioning and ventilation! Fully expected were new banks of lockers for the students, handsome new furniture in the library, carpeting throughout the building, and a completed moot courtroom, with judges' bench, witness and clerk's boxes, jury box, judges' chambers and jury room.

Instead there began the worst and most tenuous three years in the history of the law school.

Every change, every step and every purchase was a problem and a delay. As the time for the move from Point Loma approached, almost no work had been done on Cedar Street, ominous rumblings were heard everywhere, and monetary restrictions seemed to mount.

When Admiral Zumwalt changed the regulation requiring sailors to leave their ship in uniform, the so-called "locker clubs" in downtown San Diego, where the sailors had changed into civilian clothes, were going out of business and had hundreds of used lockers to sell. In June, the dean wrote a memo to university vice president Bob Dunn, indicating that in the effort to save money he had instructed me to explore the purchase of used lockers which I had found might be available at five dollars each from the 4-O Locker Club. (After further negotiations, I secured 325 lockers for $1200, or about $3.70 each—but they were a terrible mistake and were ultimately discarded when funds were available for proper ones.)

Soon faculty salaries began to be delayed, and there was nationwide publicity about the university's cash flow problems, with consequent impact on present and prospective students and faculty. Two faculty members gave notice of their departure, although public announcement of the move to first-rate facilities in downtown San Diego allayed some student concerns. There was such objection from the faculty and dean, that the university's earlier plan for the SPA to share part of the building with the law school was fortunately abandoned.

The student newspaper of April, 1973, had a large picture of the outside of the handsome building with the optimistic caption: "LAW SCHOOL SOMEDAY?"

After George Stevens left the law school, the chairmanship of the Building Committee fell to me, just in time for the final preparations to move. By then we had come to the full realization that there would be a minimum of remodeling, no new furniture, none of the dreamed-of luxuries, not even the expected necessities. But I also recognized that our move and the university's move from Point Loma was to be an every-man-for- himself situation, with no holds barred.

The dean seemed to have adopted a magnificent indifference to the problems of the move, so we proceeded without restraint. Without speaking to anyone or obtaining authority or permission from anyone, I had a check-out desk, 18 round four-person tables, 5 square four-person tables, 17 rectangular six-person tables, 11 eight-person tables, 323 chairs, 18 double carrels and 8 single carrels in the university's Ryan library stickered and tagged as going to the law school. We also tagged furniture in the university faculty lounge, tagged large pieces of blue-green carpeting, and even tagged two small pianos and two pool tables in the USIU students' lounge! (The SPA later successfully insisted we give one piano to them.)

When the trucks came to move the furniture and equipment from the law school, they were directed also to pick up all of the other tagged items—and no objection was ever raised. So it was that the new law school library actually had sufficient study tables and chairs to provide the minimum seating capacity required, there was carpeting in many areas, there was some furniture for the enormous lounge areas in the new building, a piano in the auditorium, and the student lounge on the fourth floor had two pool tables and at least a little furniture.

It was an unbelievable coincidence that a first-year student named Jim Shelger had for a short time made a living re-covering pool tables—and for the price of new green felt we purchased, Jim provided the students with the luxury of two excellent newly-covered tables! His skill and the skills later discovered of carpenters, electricians and cabinet-makers among the students gave rise to the rumor that our Admissions Committee gave special consideration to applicants' competence in any of the building trades.

Aside from the planned remodeling, such a small part of which was accomplished, the task of simply cleaning the SPA building and making it usable was awesome. Among the most difficult obstacles was the removal of the hardwood flooring and barres in the dance studios, and next the removal of the tons of discarded equipment, broken furniture, old lockers, waste and rubbish throughout the building. Black paint had to be removed from paneling and wainscoting, walls cleaned and painted, and hardware repaired.

Shortly after the actual move, there seemed no reason that Toni and I could not take our long-planned trip to the Orient, and Galinson took over as chairman of the operation. He was able to enlist the aid of Roy Bell, the Student Bar Association president, who put together a large crew of students to do the major share of the work in making the building liveable. Compensated by credit toward their tuition, the cadre of students not only performed a remarkable task at great personal sacrifice, but also built an esprit de corps which went far toward dispelling the general malaise caused by the university's financial woes and its inability to employ professional help to accomplish the remodeling of the building.

Before the beginning of the fall term some additional moneys were made available by the university, undoubtedly resulting from a luncheon among Dr. Rust, Castetter and Bell at the top of the Holiday Inn on First Avenue a block from the school. It was there that Bell bluffed a threat that the students' tuition would be put in a trust and withheld from the university unless Castetter and Rust saw to it that more of the remodeling bills were paid. The following year the Student Bar Association under Stuart Smits was not bluffing.

When we returned to San Diego from our trip, the work was still going forward at full bore and the tiered seating was being installed in one of the classrooms. The planned corridor around the library had to be abandoned for lack of funds, so the partitions were erected directly on the perimeter of the library to create the faculty offices. Fortunately the university found the money or the credit to obtain the library shelving, and it arrived in the nick of time. Miracle of miracles, the building was ready enough by the end of August to greet the new and returning students.

Chapter VIII

Turmoil Amidst Financial Woes

Rather than abating after the law school's move, the chaos of the university's financial woes continued and was even exacerbated.

Compared to the compact little building on Point Loma, the new facility seemed cavernous. The elevator was slow and felt somehow unreliable, so most everyone used the long stairways and got plenty of exercise walking from the first to the second, third and fourth floors two or three times a day. Students and faculty alike did their best to accept the many inconveniences and uncompleted remodeling, but the complaints against the law school, the university and its president grew louder each day.

Everything looked so stark and vast, and the enormous walls so bare, that I thought the general mood would be much enhanced by some aesthetic refreshment. Somewhere on the university Point Loma campus I had found a multitude of heavy, black-painted wooden picture frames, into which I put some of our old prints and engravings, as well as several etchings by WPA artists which Joe Erdelac, a former client, had given me years before. Hung all about the school, these made the rooms and hallways look much less cold. In addition, three large South American hand-woven rugs I found at Pier One, hung on long wooden spiral poles we made into drapery rods, provided warmth and interest on three of the great hallway walls.

Subjects of some controversy, dislike by many, and eventual discard were the small signs I had made for the handsome wooden doors to many of the rooms. In an effort to provide a little pseudo-culture and perhaps a bit of instant tradition, I chose several legal phrases and maxims from my Bouvier law dictionary and had small black plaques with white lettering made. *Nisi Prius Lounge* was for the stairway to the fourth floor student lounge. *Nisi Prius* is the name given the courts of general jurisdiction in England.

Among others on several classroom and activity doors were: *Ubi jus, ibi remedium* (Where there is a right, there is a remedy), *Qui bene interrogat bene docet* (He who questions well teaches well), *Accusare nemo debet se, nisi coram Deo* (No one is obliged to accuse himself, unless before God), *Ignorantia excusatur, non juris sed facti* (Ignorance of fact may excuse, but not ignorance of law), *Veritas nihil veretur nisi abscondi* (Truth fears nothing but concealment), *Aequum et bonum est lex legum* (What is just and right is the law), and *Vigilantibus et non dormientibus jura subveniunt* (The laws serve the vigilant not those who sleep).

On the second floor we created a client counseling office and observation area. Having found a one-way mirror, I had it so installed that students could conduct client interviews in a model attorney's office in apparent privacy and be observed without interference by a class in another room, the conversation being heard over a loudspeaker system.

But the project which occupied most of my leisure time was the moot courtroom. Hermann Zillgens worked with me and drew the plans, but there were no funds to accomplish their fulfillment. By the same happy chance that produced the student who could cover pool tables, we discovered that Alton (Alex) Brody, a second year student, was an accomplished cabinet-maker, Larry Petty a competent carpenter, with Phil Vinci and Dennis Callan as excellent assistants! In addition to those four, there were others more or less skilled, who helped occasionally as needed—all compensated by credit toward their tuition.

There were no funds for materials, so I advanced them in the vain hope that they would eventually be repaid—which for the most part they were, much later. Actually, for Brody and the others and me it became a labor of love, especially as we saw the room slowly take shape. The judges' bench was built on a raised platform, with the witness box somewhat lower on one side, and a place for a clerk on the other. A tiered jury box was built on one side of the "well" and a tiered section for the press on the other side. Hardwoods were used throughout.

At the Hotel del Coronado, Brody and I saw some spiral posts of the type I envisioned to support the rail separating the well from the rest of the courtroom, and took photos which we showed to various woodworking shops until we found some for our use. We also built two long, sturdy tables for counsel, with leather tops, and were able to have several old university chairs recovered, some in red and some in brown, for counsel, jurors and the press.

Alex was remarkably skilled, and took great pains to make every joint and surface as perfect as possible. However, on the few occasions when there was some slight discrepancy, he would exclaim, "Well, that's close enough for government work."

We had the great Masonic chandelier removed from the center of the ceiling and, with great difficulty, installed a round cover we had found to hide the hole which remained. To replace the lighted leaded glass window with the Masonic emblem on the side wall, I had a new leaded window made with the school's initials, designed by Mark Dennis, a most talented student, and executed by Leslie Barrett, a cousin of Steve Boudreau, another student.

On the south wall of the room there was unusually handsome high paneling which would provide an appropriate backdrop to the judges' bench. But the bench had to be built on the platform far in front of that paneling, so the only solution would have been to move the entire paneling forward some ten feet. That would not only place the paneling directly behind the bench, but would also create space behind it for a jury room. One weekend, a large crew of students was recruited, and by dint of great effort and brute strength, the entire enormous panel was moved away from the wall and forward, and there supported to create a new wall!

Ultimately, the movable bleacher stands used by the SPA were replaced with permanent tiered amphitheater desks and chairs, and the room carpeted in a deep red, making it the most beautiful and impressive law school courtroom in the country.

Some spice and variety during the dismal year were provided by Larry Lee, the recently arrived very bright and experienced teacher. He was a true free spirit who was either loved or decried by the students. He it was who was said to have shown X-rated movies at a fraternity smoker in his home, who married one of his students, and who was late in grading and once even "lost" a whole set of exams—but at the same time was often cited as an outstanding professor and the student favorite!

Joining the faculty with excellent credentials just after the move was Ralph Newman, a quiet, scholarly little man who added a new dimension during the short time he was there. He departed after only a year as the university's financial problems began affecting the faculty paychecks. Along with Stevens, Newman and Weninger who left, John Lindsey, the librarian took a year's leave of absence, filed a claim for back wages and never returned.

Everyone else on the faculty and staff chose to remain, despite the mounting problems. As our checks were delayed first a few days, then a few weeks we became not only concerned but financially strained, until Hal Stephens, the president of the Mission Federal Credit Union, devised a unique and imaginative procedure. He reached an agreement with President Rust which provided that the credit union would advance the salaries to the university employees when they were due. The university agreed to reimburse the credit union when it had the funds, within various periods agreed upon: at first ten days, then two weeks, then thirty days and even longer!

We in turn signed papers assigning each month's salary claim against the university to the credit union—and so it was that we were again paid on time, although the wages that had previously been skipped were not then repaid. Variously owed one or two months' salary, a few of us were owed for as many as three and even six months! It was not until much later that we were also to learn that the university had not made its 7.5% of base salary contributions to our TIAA-CREF pension fund, and had not even made payment of income tax, social security or 5% pension plan deductions which it had withheld.

Coincident with these troubles, it began to appear that various university creditors for law school goods and services had not been paid—among them law review and law book publishers. And soon information of the problems was bound to reach the ears of the American Bar Association and the Association of American Law Schools, which it did.

Almost like a replacement for George Stevens, another highly-regarded former Case Western Reserve professor joined the faculty that fall. Maurice Culp was an experienced teacher and administrator, having for many years been an acting dean. He served the law school well and loyally, and in tumultuous times provided sound judgment and a strong calming influence on students and faculty alike for the last few years before his death.

Somehow the law school managed to limp through the 1973-1974 school year.

It was in April of 1974 that Patty Hearst, heiress to a publishing fortune, adopted the name of Tania, the German-American mistress of the Revolutionary, Che Guevara. She had been abducted by a ragtag group calling themselves the Symbionese Liberation Army, and had herself become a foul-mouthed gun-carrying bank robber. Also in that year King Faisal of Saudi Arabia led the oil price increases which startled and froze the world. Alexander Solzhenitsyn, the great writer, began his exile as a true hero who had come to represent the conscience of Russia.

Toni and I sold a Tiffany leaded-glass lampshade given me by a client, and used the proceeds to go to Italy that summer, in the fond hope that somehow by the time of our return enough of the funds from the sale of the Point Loma campus would have been released to diminish the university's terrible cash flow problems and the creditors, including the faculty, would have been paid.

As the voyage to Italy neared its end, we essayed into Jugoslavia for a few days, marveling at the beauty of the Dalmatian coast and the ancient city/state of Dubrovnik. After returning to Bari by ferry, we boarded a train north along the eastern coast of Italy to Venice. All the stories I'd heard and pictures I'd seen of Venice were true—it was a fairyland. We rode the *vaporetti* which ply the canals like crowded buses on water and marveled at the stately buildings whose foundations were seemingly immersed in the sea.

The four magnificent gilded copper horses and the Clock Tower with the two Moors striking the hours gave me goose bumps as we sat in St. Mark's Square. We had tea in the open air listening to the strains of Verdi and Puccini played by an accomplished orchestra to audiences of carefree Venetians and tourists, and literally thousands of pigeons.

Probaby most of all we reveled in the bustle and the frenzy on the water and in the narrow streets, the Old Rialto Buildings with the fruit and vegetable markets, and the men hawking all manner of food and souvenirs as they walked up and down in front of the grand hotels like the Bauer Grunwald and the Danielli.

But from Venice we returned to the realities of home—and a crisis at the law school.

Rex Brown, a remarkably bright and able student who was the head of the Client Counseling Board, had agreed with his wife to house-sit for us while we were in Europe. The year before we had made a similar arrangement with Ted Bromfield[26] and his wife, and having a student and his wife enjoy the house and care for it in our absence had worked out so well that we had asked the Browns if they would be interested, and they were.

---

[26] Both Bromfield and Brown were outstanding students and became very successful, Brown as counsel for an oil company and a private practitioner, Bromfield as a top-ranking City Attorney.

Rex and his wife met us at the airport on our return from Europe, to take us back to our house in their Volkswagen bus. Taciturn as always, and with his brown mustache covering half his ruggedly handsome face, Rex listened quietly with me while the two women chatted in the rear seat. Satisfied that the dogs were fine and all was well at home, I then inquired of Rex: "How are things going at the law school?"

"It's closed."

"What do you mean, closed?"

"Just that. The building was closed."

It was like pulling teeth. "Where is the dean? Where are the faculty?"

Finally, he explained a little. "The dean and his wife were in Hawaii, and while he was gone the Fire Marshall simply ordered the building closed. I think the dean's back now and the first floor offices are being used, but the rest of the building is shut tight. That's really all we know."

That was the crisis to which we had returned from the beauties of Italy and Jugoslavia and the charms of Venice!

The next morning I could hardly wait to hear the full story. It soon became clear to me that for several years there had been fire code improvement requests by the city, with which Dr. Rust, as was his wont, had several times promised to comply. Since nothing had been done as promised throughout the period of the occupancy of the building by the SPA however, the axe had finally fallen during the law school's tenancy.

The Fire Marshall had not only ordered the building closed and the promised improvements completed, but had upgraded the requirements on the basis that a law school had more seated classes than the School for Performing Arts, and more stringent fire precautions were therefore necessary. Responding to urgent pleas he did agree to allow the use of the library and offices on the lower and main floors, without which the school's operation would have been completely impossible.

It fell to architect Dick Lareau to prepare the most desirable and least expensive remodeling plans which would satisfy the Fire Marshal's requirements. Pending their completion and approval, the dean and Stuart Smits, president of the Student Bar Association, had taken the first most important step of finding available space in which classes could be held. Fortunately, a deal was made for the use of rooms in the San Diego Community Concourse, only a few blocks from the school. Classes were conducted there until enough of the remodeling work was completed to persuade the Fire Marshall to permit the use of the upper floors of the law school building.

The availability of money from the university was once again the major factor in the law school's welfare. The total cost of the remodel was to be in the neighborhood of $200,000, and since the school's financial problems were common knowledge, the contractor insisted that a substantial cash sum be on deposit in trust before work would begin.

That summer the Student Bar Association had actually negotiated an agreement with the university reminiscent of the threat of the previous year. Tuition money was to be put into an escrow account to assure the purchase of the necessary court reports, law reviews and book supplements for the law school library. The students had entered the negotiations when they realized that the embattled university was not maintaining the library according to accepted standards. Pursuant to the agreement, $110,000 collected from tuition receipts for the fall of 1974 went into escrow, with $25,000 added in January from spring tuition.

From those library funds, the students and the university agreed that $26,000 be released to the contractor toward payment for the even greater priority of the required remodeling. In addition, great good fortune was provided by John Cranston, the attorney who had for years been a member of the USIU Board of Trustees and a good friend to the law school. It was he who obtained a personal loan from his bank and loaned sufficient additional moneys to the university to satisfy the contractor's requirements and allow the work to go forward.

An outside fire escape from the third to the second floor was to be built, and large glass partitions installed at the head of each flight of stairs inside, as well as many other changes such as fire doors, emergency lighting and new fire extinguishers throughout. At the very last minute, the Community Concourse rooms having been previously booked for a conference beginning November 4, the all-powerful Fire Marshall gave his conditional O.K. to the resumption of classes in the building on Cedar Street—much to the relief of both faculty and students.

But until the outside fire escape and all of the partitions were installed and fully completed, the condition imposed by the Fire Marshall was incredibly onerous—he required that the school have three fire guards on two shifts to patrol the second, third and fourth floors to be sure the students could get out of the building in case of fire!

Not only was that requirement outrageous in that it applied safety standards meant for young school children and not for adults, but because it added greatly to the financial burden the university could ill afford, and those uniformed men were a constant and depressing daily reminder of our troubles.

After the work was completed, many found fault aesthetically with the front fire escapes and the blocking of the imposing staircases, formerly open and unobstructed. But we were at least glad that Lareau had found a way to design the stair partitions of glass, making them as unobtrusive as possible, and happy most of all that another ordeal was behind us.

But the law school's problems did not end with the resumption of classes in the building. Instead they were ever mounting. The Accreditation Committee of the Association of American Law Schools, having learned of the delinquent faculty salaries as well as the Fire Marshall problems, had indicated their desire for an accreditation visitation both by them and the American Bar Association. Even prior to that request for a visitation, there was a greater problem unknown to the faculty—the law school had already been warned of the possibility of an order requiring the school to show cause why it should not be disaccredited by the ABA!

At the same time conversations had been begun to seek a merger with Hastings College of Law, a part of the University of California system. There was precedent for the idea of Hastings in San Diego, since as recently as 1972 both houses of the California legislature had passed a bill to establish a Hastings law school campus in San Diego—which was vetoed by then Governor Ronald Reagan.

The figure of two and a half million dollars had somehow been arrived at as an amount believed to be acceptable to Dr. Rust for the purchase of the school and the amount considered appropriate by the Hastings people. The prospects for such a merger were for a short time undoubtedly helpful with the accreditation problems as well as holding out some possible hope of a brighter future for the faculty and the students.

A very impressive committee was formed to promote the merger on behalf of California Western, including Judge Richard Ault and influential attorney "Red" Boudreau, and led by Paul Peterson, another prominent San Diego attorney. Working effectively with them was Gary Hunt, a politically savvy law student who was able to persuade Senator Moscone to sponsor a bill in the State Senate and Assemblyman Larry Kapiloff to sponsor a bill in the Assembly to merge California Western and Hastings College of Law.

Both the then unaccredited Western State law college and the law school of the University of San Diego mounted strong opposition to the merger, the latter even going so far as to have its dean testify in one of the Assembly committee meetings before which I had been asked to appear. Many color slides had been prepared of both the interior and exterior of the Cedar Street building. These were thrown on a screen in the darkened meeting room as I made comments and described them to the committee.

There were murmurs of approval at the pictures of the building's exterior, and louder sounds of surprise at the beauty of the moot courtroom. Dean Weckstein of the University of San Diego gave some sort of grunt. When the photo of a paneled office with attractive paintings on the walls was flashed on the screen, I said, "This is a faculty office on the main floor of the building."

"Oh, sure," snorted Weckstein.

"Yes, Dean, and I'd prefer that you refrain from any more derogatory sounds or suggestions challenging these photos or my integrity. This photograph is of my own faculty office."

That particular committee voted in favor of the bill, but unfortunately the appropriations committee of the Senate later voted it down. The dream of a merger with Hastings was, at least for that year, dead. In view of the general anti-lawyer, tax-saving and anti-government climate in California at the time, especially in the legislature, most of us were not really surprised. There was a truly valiant effort made by many lawyers, judges, legislators and laymen, who were supporters of California Western. In addition there were many others, including alumni of both schools, who believed that there should be another state-supported law school in southern California. They believed, very rightly, that the merger of Hastings and California Western would have provided the easiest and least expensive method of accomplishing that end. But it was not to be.

Castetter had in the past talked a few times about wishing the law school could be governed by a "separate Board of Trustees," but his thoughts never seemed focused on how that could be accomplished nor did he ever say how he thought that would in any way alleviate or improve the university's and hence the law school's financial problems. But in any event nothing ever came of such talk, and nothing was done.

The law school faculty had all been strongly in favor of the Hastings connection, but not so with respect to Castetter's next effort. The dean had approached Gordon Shaber, the dean of McGeorge Law School of the University of the Pacific. The faculty first learned of the effort when the Shaber brothers (the dean's younger brother was the business manager, I believe) arrived in the building for an inspection, and were introduced.

There were immediate questions and doubts. Whereas Hastings was a prestigious law school and a part of the University of California, with its obvious financial stability, McGeorge was altogether different. A proprietary night school prior to its affiliation with the University of the Pacific, McGeorge was only then slowly gaining respectability. By dint of extreme concentration on the California Bar exam, McGeorge graduates had been able to achieve a remarkably high Bar passage rate. This had served to provide the school with almost instant recognition and respect.

Neverthless, the California Western faculty was fearful of the prospect of a McGeorge affiliation. Many were concerned with its financial strength, what would be done about their delinquent salaries, about the TIAA-CREF and Social Security withholdings, and even about the general reputation of McGeorge.

After Shaber had been told by Marvin Anderson, the Hastings dean, that McGeorge was free to negotiate with USIU, McGeorge reached the figure of $1,500,000 as their evaluation of California Western's assets. Whether or not Dr. Rust would have considered that figure is not known, nor were the concerns of the faculty ever addressed, for early in the summer of 1975, Castetter was notified that the University of the Pacific was not interested in pursuing the matter.

The ABA-AALS inspection, which Dean Castetter had successfully delayed until after the law school again had the full use of its building, was held in early December of 1974. The inspection team reported on the delinquent faculty salaries and pension fund deficits, as well as other debts and deep financial problems of the university. It reported that the library's 45,675 volumes was well below the AALS recommendation of 60,000, that it was short of the minimum annual recommended appropriations, and that there was a serious lack of continuations, supplements and replacements. The report stated that the law school was not operating in compliance with ABA standards of approval and recommended that appropriate steps be taken by the Council of the Section on Legal Education—and a Commission was formed to consider such action!

In March of 1975, the dean was notified of the Commission's findings and "advised" that unless certain conditions were met (which were impossible) all applicants for admission to the class entering in September, 1975, whether or not they had indicated acceptance of admission, should be advised in writing that the law school's accreditation was being reviewed by the American Bar Association pursuant to a resolution of the Council of the Section on Legal Education and Admissions to the Bar which directs the law school to show cause why the American Bar Association should not withdraw accreditation from the law school. The dean was requested also similarly to advise the faculty in writing.

The dean decided to ignore the "advice" he received, choosing to consider it to be the view of the writer of the letter and not an authorized mandate. There can be no doubt of the deleterious effect the giving of such notice to each law school applicant would have had. How different the law school's history might have been had Castetter capitulated.

Even without knowing of the law school's precarious accreditation position, the mood of students and faculty was dark and pessimistic indeed. Castetter and Rust, but primarily Rust, were portrayed as the villains. Many members of the faculty openly condemned Rust to the students as a wrongdoer, even an embezzler, and were vehement in their criticism of the university—apparently overlooking the fact that the law school was a part of it.

No thought seemed to be given that the university was a business, and that businesses often have problems or fail by reason of bad management and innumerable other factors. The general attitude seemed to be that unless someone, presumably Dr. Rust, had stolen or embezzled or committed some other wrong, an entity like a university could not have financial difficulties. It was simply inconceivable and unacceptable that faculty salaries and necessary school expenses not be paid. It almost seemed to be the general consensus that the receipt of faculty salaries and benefits was sacrosanct, not at all like the salaries of ordinary businesses.

Fortunately, the Mission Federal Credit Union board in January, 1975, had authorized payroll loans up to $300,000, which fully covered the law school faculty through its darkest months. Such loans to the university continued for many years, reaching $1.2 million secured by a trust deed on 54 acres of university property in 1981, and to $2.5 million by 1987. In July, 1991, USIU filed for Chapter 11 reorganization, a 26-acre parcel was sold at auction, and ultimately in October, 1993, the loan was paid in full.

Chapter IX

Agreement For Sale and Academic Consortium

Amidst all the doom and gloom, the future looked bleak for the school and for all of us. Four of the faculty had already left, others were unsure what course to take. The dean, for the first time since he had come to California Western, had arranged to teach a summer course at Hastings. Toni and I began to consider our options, but always came back to the same thought: that our present situation, my teaching law in San Diego, was what we most wanted.

As a result, my thoughts all centered on what I might do to preserve the law school as a viable institution and be able to continue to live in La Jolla and teach law.

Several law schools in the country had merged with universities, all sorts of businesses merge or are bought out, businesses are regularly spun off or sold—but to my knowledge there was no precedent for a law school to be spun off or sold by a university. But the more I thought about it, the more I believed it might be accomplished. I approached the dean.

"Dean, the prospects of Hastings or McGeorge or any other merger really seem very unlikely to me. Would you object to my talking to Dr. Rust and trying to figure out a way to buy the law school from USIU?"

"Where would you get the money?"

"I have to work out a way to do it without money. It is now our great good luck that we're not on the campus but in a downtown building, so I think it's possible."

"Go ahead. Right now I see very little hope. And I know Bully Bill—he'll never agree to anything. I don't think you have a chance."

Night after night I pondered the matter, sitting at our dining room table writing various scenarios and possibilities. It had been more than six years since I had left the practice of law, and it was actually rejuvenating to feel like a lawyer again, seeking to solve a client's problem. Slowly a feasible solution began to take shape in my mind and I called Bob Dunn, the USIU vice president whom I knew. Bob had been a practicing lawyer before he joined the university, and I felt he might be most receptive to my approach.

We arranged to meet for lunch at the La Jolla Village Inn, and there I outlined to him my ideas for the purchase of the law school by a new non-profit corporation.

"It looks to me, Bob, that this may be the only way financially to save the law school, and certainly the only way to preserve it as a fully accredited school. Do you think Dr. Rust would be willing to listen?"

"Yes, I think maybe he would. As you know, despite all the problems and all the bad things said about him, dreamer that he is, good education and scholarship are his primary goals, and he's often told me how much he wants the law school to succeed. Let me talk to him and see what he says. I'll call if he's willing to meet with you."

Not long afterwards Dunn called to tell me that Rust had agreed to meet, and a time and date not in conflict with his frantic schedule was arranged. I told the dean.

"Don't get your hopes up—and don't trust anything he says. But keep me informed as you go."

At our first meeting, with Bob Dunn present, Rust was remarkably cordial and receptive. Prior to that time, I had had very little contact with him. We had talked alone once for a few minutes before I joined the law school, but after that our contacts had been rare and formal—the relationship of a fairly new and junior professor to the president of the university, and a somewhat imperious president at that!

After I had recited to Dr. Rust the precarious position that I believed the law school to be in, facts he was more familiar with than I was, I presented a broad outline of my ideas.

"It seems to me that the only solution to the situation would be for the law school to go its own way. The law school should be purchased from the university by a separate corporation which would relieve the university of all those of its debts which arose from the law school operation."

"You mean the school would become a proprietary institution for profit?"

"Oh, no. It would be a non-profit corporation which would assume the university's law-school debts, removing them from your balance sheet."

"But the university would lose what I consider one of its jewels, and the law school assets would be off our balance sheet."

"We could work out a purchase price which, with the assumption of debt, would not affect your balance sheet. Or actually, depending on the cost figures on your books, it may improve it. But much more important I think for you now, is that the university would be relieved of the pressure of a large number of very troublesome current creditors whose claims are in arrears. The new corporation would agree to pay the assumed debts out of its operating income, and give a note to the university payable over a period of time for the balance of the purchase price over the amount of the assumed debts.

"And in my judgment, Dr. Rust, this would be the only hope of preventing the law school's losing its accreditation with the ABA—which I know you would want to prevent in every way possible."

"By golly, Mr. Gafford, this may deserve some thought. Work with Bob on it and put something down on paper for me to look at. You surely don't sound like most professors I've known."

Dunn and I met once or twice more to ponder the possibilities. I told Castetter about the meeting, but said nothing to anyone else. Thinking it best not to mention it to the faculty for several reasons, I did all the work on the several drafts of a suggested contract at home. Without a secretary or a dictating machine with which I'd been familiar for so many years, and long before the day of the presently ubiquitous and irreplaceable word processor, I worked with sharp pencils and sheets of my old law firm stationery.

When I told Castetter the broad outlines of what I planned to propose, he began to sound disturbed and said that I had to keep Ralph Miller fully informed and include him in all negotiations. Miller had been a friend of Castetter since their days on the faculty together at San Diego State, had a successful tax and probate law firm, and had been an adjunct tax professor and good friend to the law school.

But that presented a problem. When I told Rust that Castetter wanted Miller included in all our meetings, Rust (by reason of some past relationship of which I was unaware) said he refused to participate in any meetings with "that man." As a result, it was then arranged that one Mike Zaden, a clerk in Miller's office, was to attend our meetings. A young man who had not yet passed the Bar, Zaden may have kept Miller apprised of the proceedings, but he could add little himself. He did provide the conduit to his office where much of the typing and other clerical work required for the documentation of the transaction was performed.

Jon Chester, a very bright tax attorney and alumnus of California Western, was an associate in the Miller firm and handled the incorporation on June 3, 1975, of the new non-profit corporation, California Western School of Law, which was used as the legal entity which was to purchase the law school from USIU.[27] The new corporation had all the degree-granting rights of the often-amended San Diego Chiropractic College charter.

---

[27] Chester also made substantial contribution of his legal expertise during the early days of the new corporation. Although Mike Zeden, as assistant secretary of the corporation was a signatory of the eventual contract of sale, it was later reported that he left the firm before he had passed the Bar.

Early in the negotiations, Dr. Rust was concerned, and told me his Board of Trustees would be very concerned about the future operation of the law school and the make-up of the proposed purchasing corporation.

"Are you going to be the dean of the new school?"

"Oh, absolutely not. To my mind the continuity of the school with as little change as possible is our most important job. Being a dean is the least of my desires, and I doubt the faculty would want me."

"What assurance do we have that we are not being asked to sell this fine institution to a group who will ruin it or operate it for profit?"

"Basically, only my assurance that I can and will prevent it. Certainly I do not want to teach at a proprietary school or an unaccredited school. That's the purpose of this whole exercise."

"That's true, and I'd accept your assurance—but you know, maybe losing accreditation would not be all that bad. I could operate the school the way Western State is operated—lower the admission requirements, open a night school, double the enrollment and make a real profit."

By that time, after so many meetings, the early stiff formality of our relationship had gone and we were on a first-name basis.

"You say that, Bill, but I know you don't mean it. Nothing you've ever done would suggest that you'd permit, let alone foster lower educational standards."

"Well, let's go on for now. We've not yet talked about the purchase price. What do you have in mind?"

"The figure used in the Hastings effort, which you knew and I assume was acceptable to you, was two and a half million. But so far that looks unlikely. In Castetter's discussions with McGeorge of the University of the Pacific, which you may not know, McGeorge's evaluation was one and a half million. My thought is that our figure should be somewhere between those two."

"Why?"

"Because it must be low enough to give the new entity a real chance of survival, but high enough that there can be no credible claim that it was a transfer in fraud of creditors."

Rust flared. "What do you mean, fraud? We're certainly not talking about any fraud."

"If the university were to transfer away a valuable asset at less than what it is reasonably worth, any one of the legion of the university's creditors could assert that they were improperly deprived of the right to look to that asset to satisfy their claim. They would allege that it is what is called in law a transfer in fraud of creditors and seek to block it."

"I understand."

"From all the numbers that we've talked about, the balance due Connecticut Mutual on the building mortgage, to Cubic Corporation, to Daley, to the trade creditors, to the pension fund, to the faculty, possibly even to HEW, and whatever part of your debt to the Union Bank that we could assume, one million seven hundred and fifty thousand dollars is as much as could possibly be handled—and it seems to me would be a number safe against being successfully attacked."

Dr. Rust and Bob Dunn and I spent a great deal of time working around that number and many other difficult problems, including how the balance of the amount due the university after the assumption of the debts would be paid, which university debt payments by the new corporation would be credited toward its note to the university, what would happen if any creditor refused to accept the assumption of the debt by the new entity, how the transaction could be undone in the event of a sale to either Hastings or McGeorge, and how the very troublesome "federal interest" of the Department of Health, Education and Welfare would be handled.

During the negotiations, I often talked with Castetter to try to determine from him some of the budget figures I needed to be able to determine how much money after operating expenses would be available for the various payments to be made. It soon became evident that the dean of a school controlled by a university headed by

Dr. Rust had been privy to few financial details, and separating law school costs from university-supplied services was extremely difficult. As a result many of the calculations had to be guesses or best estimates.

At one of the many early meetings with Rust, I voiced a deep concern.

"One thing has been really worrying me, Bill, which we haven't talked about. What I'm afraid of is that handling this as I'm proposing, as a straight purchase of assets by a new corporation, what will prevent the ABA or the AALS, or even more immediately, HEW, from saying this is a new law school? If they do, we'd have to start from scratch for completely new accreditation—with all the forms and meetings and hearings and time that would be involved. If we lost the immediate GI Bill availability to our students, it would be fatal!"

"There's a solution to that. Call the deal a consortium, George. No one really knows what a consortium is."

That turned out to be a life-saving suggestion. After many earlier drafts, my hand-written contract which as later refined became the first purchase in the nation of a law school from a university, was titled "Sale and Consortium Agreement"! It recited that it was "...the mutual desire of the parties to remain related in a Consortium to assure the maintenance of academic quality, maintain costs at economically feasible levels through the common use of facilities and expertise of the parties, and provide through the cooperation of the parties educational and financial opportunities for the students of the parties through means of central registration and control."

It recited further that it was the "...desire of USIU to sell and of California Western to purchase all of the land, building, library, furniture, fixtures, publications, trade marks[28], lists, files, applications and any and all other property, both tangible and intangible, presently used by the law school located at 350 Cedar Street..."

---

[28] This later became important when we sought to enjoin a correspondence school from using the name California Western University.

It provided that all tuition income from and after June 1, 1975, would be paid to California Western and that after the closing date of the transaction, California Western would assume the obligations of USIU set forth in the agreement. The assumption of the obligations, all long term, and the giving of a non-negotiable 7% promissory note by California Western to USIU for the balance of the purchase price, against which would be credited all payments of delinquent faculty salaries, pension and accrued sabbatical payments and law school bills, was the concept which made possible the purchase of the law school without any cash.

It was also provided that in the event that the negotiations between USIU and Hastings or McGeorge should result in the merger of the law school into one of them within 120 days of the date of the agreement, California Western would convey all of the property to that purchaser and would be relieved of all its obligations under the agreement.

There were provisions for a Consortium Committee to set general consortium policies and a staff to perform the administrative work involved in registration of students, maintenance of transcripts, billing and accounting, payroll, etc. at a cost to California Western limited to a small percentage of tuition income. But either party had the right to withdraw from the Academic Consortium by unilateral action after October 1, 1976.

As we came closer and closer to agreement on the terms of the contract, Castetter's view of a successful conclusion to my negotiations was unchanged.

"Bill Rust will never sign away the law school. I know Bully Bill!"

"We'll see," I replied.

"He won't do it. He'll find a way to get out of it," Castetter insisted.

On June 8, 1975, the "Agreement for Sale and Academic Consortium" was signed by William C. Rust as president and Robert S. Dunn as secretary of USIU, and by Robert Castetter as president and Michael E. Zaden as assistant secretary of California Western School of Law.

After the signing, Castetter insisted, again with knowing certainty: "Rust will never go through with it and transfer all the assets to the new corporation. He'll never give up the income from the law school."

All I could do was smile and nod, and hope he was wrong. Indeed, there was yet a great deal to be done, and the road ahead was still rocky. Not long afterwards, Castetter went to Hastings law school in San Francisco as had previously been arranged, and any contacts with him during the period of the difficult preparations for the closing of the transaction had to be by telephone.

One of the first hurdles appeared very soon. A delegation of four of my colleagues on the faculty came into my office one afternoon. Tom Coyne was the spokesman at first. He was a very able young professor, and one of the faculty members most hostile to both Castetter and Rust because of the financial problems, but particularly critical and distrusting of Rust.

He began in a somewhat confrontational mode. "We've heard rumors, George, that you've been involved in some sort of dealings on behalf of the law school with the university."

"Yes, I have."

"Well, I'm not necessarily saying we wouldn't want you to represent us, but we have the right to be consulted and to decide whether we do or not."

"You may be right, but I don't feel that I have been acting as counsel to the faculty. I've had little faith in the success of the merger of the law school with either Hastings or McGeorge, so with the dean's permission, I've been exploring the possibility on my own of the purchase of the school from the university."

"You mean you want to buy the law school?"

"Oh, no. The buyer would be a non-profit corporation."

"Why haven't we been informed or consulted?"

"Well, really, for several reasons. Too many participants usually make any negotiation tougher. I was struggling with a real long shot and didn't want it to interfere with the pending Hastings or

McGeorge efforts. Besides, I didn't want to get anyone's hopes up and affect any other plans you may want to make."

There seemed to be some anger, some curiosity. There were more questions.

"I've tried to devise a deal whereby the law school will be purchased by a non-profit corporation without any cash being involved, but with the assumption of several of the university's debts. The law school will be on its own, with all of its income being used only for the law school and no part of it going to a university."

"What about the faculty?"

"You can be sure that the faculty must be protected. We'd be masters of our own fate and we'd have all the income from the law school to pay delinquent salaries and see that all bills are paid on time in the future. And most important of all, there would be faculty governance."

With my last words, the tension became noticeably less.

Someone else spoke up. "But why shouldn't this all be done openly, with all of us kept fully informed?"

"Frankly, Jim, this is touchy. Some faculty members have talked of taking legal action against the university, one or two have made other moves, and I don't want this thing upset."

"How could it be upset?"

"Very easily. Some lawyer could easily advise almost any creditor actually to take personal advantage of the situation by filing or simply threatening to file a lawsuit seeking to enjoin the transfer, alleging that it would be a transfer in fraud of creditors, and insist on being paid immediately in full. And the minute we'd try to pay off one, the lid would be off, there would be many others and the deal would be impossible. And of course the mere filing of a suit would immediately prevent the transfer of clear title to the building.

"Now you four know—and by God, none of you better think of doing anything or make it possible for someone else to."

That seemed to mollify all of them, and the conversation immediately became completely collegial as I told them of many of the provisions of the projected purchase. They all indicated their hope that perhaps there could be some optimism for the future after all, wished me good luck and left my office. And I know that no faculty member betrayed my confidence.

However, on June 25, 1975, an inconceivable article appeared in the San Diego morning paper—followed by an even more inaccurate account in the evening paper.

The San Diego *Union* headline was "Western School of Law Breaks Connection With USIU's Campus". It said: "The split, which will result in fiscal independence and a separate governing board for the downtown San Diego law school, was confirmed last night by Robert K. Castetter, law school dean, and Ralph Gano Miller, a private attorney and instructor at the school."

The article continued by saying: "The two men, who were instrumental in *initiating and completing negotiations with USIU President William C. Rust*[29], said there are mutual advantages to the law school's separation from the general campus, which has been experiencing troubles over the past several years."

Even now, more than twenty-five years later, my remembered incredulity returns.

The article said that the exact cost of the "separation" was not known, but that the indications were that it would be somewhere under $2.5 million. (The exact price of the purchase had of course been completely agreed upon in the June 8 contract: $1.75 million.) Miller reportedly said that final escrow on the transaction should be completed within ten days (which with so much yet to be done was neither feasible nor possible). It was further reported that for all practical purposes the school had been an independent entity for more than four weeks (under the terms of the contract only the tuition income after June 1 was to go to the new corporation).

The article in the evening paper referred to a three-person temporary board of trustees and quoted Miller as saying "We're in the process of developing a proper kind of board so that it (Cal Western) will have the best community support." It was further reported that an

---

[29] Italics added

IRS lien was among the liens against USIU which were being assumed, and that Miller, Castetter and Jon Chester would be meeting with other creditors to determine how much debt would be shouldered by the new law school management!

This despite the fact that in the fully-negotiated contract USIU specifically agreed to save California Western harmless of any claim of the IRS, and provided the precise amounts of the debts to the four named major creditors which were to be assumed by the new corporation.

The article went on to report that USIU's original response to the proposal for an independent law school was to suggest a board made up mostly of USIU trustees, which suggestion was thrown into the wastepaper basket. The article continued by saying : "The contract signed June 15 with Rust now provides for no USIU trustees on the new board." (The date of the contract was of course June 8, and there was certainly no mention in it of the trustees of the law school corporation.)

Immediately upon reading the first article in the morning I telephoned Castetter in San Francisco—in absolute disbelief.

"Now, don't get all excited, George."

"Not get excited? The stuff in that article is outrageous, and you must know it. And what's even worse, it could destroy the whole deal. As you know, if some creditor sues to enjoin, the entire transaction would be held up because the title company would not guarantee good title. Fortunately, the facts as reported are fuzzy enough that I hope to God no one will realize it's a sale of assets which could be enjoined."

"Well, let's hope so. There was nothing I could do. Miller wanted to report it and that was the newspaper's interpretation I guess."

The next two months were busy and difficult. One of my first tasks was to procure the consent of Connecticut Mutual Life Insurance Company, the holder of the first trust deed on the law school property, to the assumption of the obligation. Counsel for the company was

Miles Harvey[30], a partner in Luce, Forward, Hamilton and Scripps, a leading San Diego law firm. The negotiations with him went smoothly and led to the acceptance by Connecticut of the law school corporation's assumption of USIU's obligation.

The second trust deed on the property was held by the Cubic Corporation, headed by Walter Zable, who had been a supporter of Dr. Rust and a member of the USIU Board of Trustees. The effort to achieve that desired agreement to release USIU and accept the assumption of the large obligation by California Western was more difficult. Their general counsel was William Bruner, and he had some concern about the approval of his Board because of USIU's serious delinquency and my seeking a more favorable payment schedule. Ultimately, Bruner confirmed to me by letter that Cubic would agree to accept our assumption without acceleration of their note, with semi-annual payments by us beginning on September 30. Interest was set at 8%.

As the pieces were slowly falling into place and Castetter had returned from his stay in San Francisco at Hastings, he began to be less openly pessimistic about the success of my endeavors. He never seemed fully to accept the transaction as a sale of assets, still continued to refer to the "disaffiliation" and a "separate Board", and began to act nervous about my actions. It was later suggested that he might have been concerned that I was seeking to replace him as dean of the new school. That could explain his apparent insistence on Ralph Miller's nominal participation in the negotiations and the report to the newspapers.

"Do you know, Dean, Rust told me that for their own satisfaction his Board would like me to furnish him before the closing the names of the members of our Board of Trustees. I told him I'd be able to give him a list of names from which a Board of seven would be chosen. So we should come up with some names, and we ought to start actually forming the Board now."

---

[30] Only a few years before, Harvey had been the successful civilian counsel for Comdr. Lloyd M. Bucher, in the Naval Inquiry into Bucher's actions as commanding officer of the unarmed U. S. intelligence ship "Pueblo", captured by the North Koreans.

Castetter gave me some names and I offered some, and together we had an impressive list (really sort of a wish list) which I prepared and delivered to Rust. Named were Roger Traynor, former Justice of the California Supreme Court, Court of Appeal Judges Richard Ault and Robert Kingsley, Federal Judge Leland Nielsen, Superior Court Judge Eli Levenson, attorneys John Barrett, Alec Cory, Ralph Miller and Paul Peterson, businessmen Gordon Luce, George Osborn and Hamilton Marston, law school deans Samuel Thurman and Robert Castetter, and Reverend Clark McElmury.

"Now we have the list, Dean, but we really have to replace the straw men in Miller's office in the incorporation papers and get started. Do you want to approach some of the people on the list or should I?"

"Why don't you do it. You know the judges from your trial practice program, and you can explain it all better than I can."

Because I thought he was already the best friend of the law school, Clark McElmury was my first effort. A retired Episcopalian minister, he had known Castetter for years and was well known to many of the faculty. When I telephoned him he immediately offered to come to our house to talk. After I had explained the purchase agreement, what we were doing and what our hopes were for a free-standing law school, he asked only a very few questions, none about personal liability.

"I'd not only be happy to serve on the first Board of Trustees, George, but I'd be honored."

But after McElmury, the road was less smooth. Federal Judge Howard Turrentine, not on the list but eminently acceptable, was the first judge I talked to, and one of his early questions was whether we had officers' and directors' liability insurance. He demurred as soon as I said we did not, and said all the other judges would too. He told me that two San Diego judges had been on a charitable board of some sort, an orphanage I believe it was, and had been named defendants in a lawsuit. There had been no insurance and even though they had prevailed in the suit, they had had to bear the expense of their defense, and every judge in San Diego knew about it.

It was clearly incumbent upon me to procure liability insurance promptly. Among the tasks I had performed in preparing for the closing of the law school purchase had been the transfer of all of the casualty insurance policies. I had dealt with Paul Schminke, an experienced insurance agent, and we had become friendly. After I had posed the need for officers' and directors' liability insurance to him, he told me that every company he had contacted had the same rule: no such insurance to a corporation unless it has been in operation for at least one year. What to do?

A week or two later Paul asked me to stop at his office. He showed me a listing in a book he had found of an insurance company that specialized in insurance for school boards.

"I'm sure their specialty must be public school boards, but what do you say we try them?"

"Hell, yes. This may save us. What do you need from me?"

We put together the information that was needed and he made the application. Within a week he called to tell me we were all set, he had a binder from the CNA Insurance Company in his hands.

Without losing any time, I renewed my trustee search by calling on Judges Nielsen, Turrentine again, Ault, and Levenson. Despite my best sales effort, both Nielsen and Turrentine gracefully declined. After long discussions with them both, with many questions about the entire purchase transaction and the obligations of the law school and of its trustees, Judges Ault and Levenson accepted. Thus it was that the first true acting Board consisted of Richard Ault, Eli Levenson, Robert Castetter, Clark McElmury, Ralph Miller and Jon Chester.

To Dr. Rust, one of the most attractive aspects of my plan to purchase the law school had been our assumption of some of USIU's debt to the Union Bank, which was seriously in arrears and was in the area of one million dollars as I recall. We had spent considerable time in determining how much of that debt could be comfortably handled by the law school as well as what amount would most benefit the university. It had been determined that $400,000 was the optimum figure, which was provided for in the agreement of sale, and I had spoken often and corresponded with Rodney Allen, a vice-president at the Union Bank headquarters office.

The bank had to be persuaded that it would be to its advantage to have the obligation of California Western, even though it was a new entity, and substitute it for $400,000 of the delinquent USIU loan on its books. When Allen had indicated that the bank would be amenable, I asked Castetter and Chester to accompany me to Los Angeles, and a tentative agreement was reached which Allen subsequently confirmed to me by letter agreement.

The bank wanted a five-year note, but agreed to allow us to pay only the interest for the first year, and thereafter to make payments of just one-tenth of the principal balance each year, payable quarterly. In what I then believed to be a real coup, Allen agreed to charge us not the then standard high fixed rate but a lower variable rate of only 1% over the bank's prime rate charged to large corporate borrowers for short-term unsecured loans. That turned out not at all to be an achievement but a real mistake on my part when the prime rate spiraled a few years later! Fortunately by then the balance had been very substantially reduced. As security, the bank was given a third trust deed on the building and a lien on the chattel property, although at my insistence the library was excluded.

Because I believed they knew him or had some other entrée, the university debt to Daley was handled by Castetter and Chester, and resulted in the agreed-upon assumption by California Western at the same 10% interest rate as Daley's USIU note, plus a separate note for the delinquent accrued interest.

Only the "federal interest" of HEW was allowed to remain in limbo pending its solution about a year later. That "federal interest" had arisen as the result of a government loan of $207,465 to USIU at the time of the remodeling of the 350 Cedar Street building for use by the School for Performing Arts. It would automatically expire after twenty years unless the building were sold to a non-eligible institution. We had made provision in the purchase agreement, as well as in a separate agreement covering the possibility of HEW's refusal to accept California Western as such eligible and successor institution.

We later learned that if the building were sold for more than its appraised value at the time of the government loan, the government would participate in any profit. In the original June 8, 1975, contract the value we had placed on USIU's interest in the building, exclusive of the federal interest, was a purely arbitrary figure of $1,000,000, with $750,000 on everything else. Accordingly, I prepared a corrective amendment, coincidentally dated exactly a year later, to reflect more accurate valuations of $1,000,000 for the library, $282,465 for furniture, fixtures and equipment, and $467,535 for the building—thereby allaying any possible problem of an assertion that a profit had been made on the sale of the building.

But there were in August of 1975 still many last-minute calculations and provisos which had to be completed before the actual closing of the long-awaited purchase could take place. It was determined, for example, that the university was in arrears for over $47,000 in TIAA-CREF (pension fund) contributions, well over $82,000 in accrued payroll and expense accounts (including quite a bit owed to Castetter, Lay and me), almost $50,000 in accrued sabbatical leaves, plus FICA, FUTA, Blue Cross and life insurance, for all of which provision had to be made.

In addition, typed at home on my old portable typewriter at the eleventh hour, was a letter agreement providing for the establishment of a "Special law school faculty payroll account." Out of funds due from California Western to USIU for operating expenses from June through August, 1975, there were to be deposited sums sufficient to pay one month's delinquent salaries to the faculty (including taxes and fringe benefits), as well as funds for additional two months' salaries for professors Ralph Newman and John Lindsey, plus such additional amounts as would be necessary to prevent legal action by Houston Lay, Lawrence Lee or John Lindsey. Those four faculty members had not been among those with whom I had talked in my office and who had in effect agreed not to try to use any last-minute leverage to their own advantage. No other creditors of the university took or threatened legal action.

On August 23, 1975, having survived what were apparently insurmountable obstacles, the "Agreement for Sale and Academic Consortium" closed, and for the first time in the nation, a law school accredited by the American Bar Association and a member of the Association of American Law Schools purchased itself from a university. California Western School of Law, an independent non-profit corporation, owned the law school and all its assets, real and personal—showing a net worth on its first balance sheet of $9,089.91!

SALE AND CONSORTIUM AGREEMENT

THIS AGREEMENT, made and entered into this — day of May, 1975, by and between United States International University of California, San Diego, California, hereinafter referred to as "USIU", and California Western School of Law, a California non-profit corporation, of San Diego, California, hereinafter referred to as "California Western,"

WITNESSETH:

WHEREAS, it is the mutual desire of the parties to be independent in the proprietorship of assets and the control of income and expense, and

WHEREAS, it is the mutual desire of the parties to remain related in a Consortium to assure the maintenance of academic quality, maintain costs at economically feasible levels through the common use of facilities and expertise of the parties, and provide through the cooperation of the parties educational and financial

Page 1 of hand-written draft of purchase—with consortium

The first time ever that a university sells its law school

opportunities for students of the parties through means of central registration and control, and

← WHEREAS, it is the desire of USIU to sell and of California Western to purchase all of the land, building, library, furniture, fixtures, publications, trade marks, lists, files, applications and any and all other property, both tangible and intangible, presently used by the law school located at 350 Cedar Street, San Diego, California,

NOW THEREFORE, in consideration of the mutual covenants of the parties and other good and valuable consideration, it is by them hereby mutually agreed as follows:

1. USIU does hereby grant and convey by warranty deed sell and to California Western the land and building located at 350 Cedar Street, City of San Diego, San Diego County, State of California, free and clear of all encumbrances except those specifically set forth in Schedule A attached hereto and made a part hereof.

2. USIU does hereby agree to sell & and transfer by warranty bill of sale, all of the furniture, fixtures, library and any and all other personal property, tangible and intangible, presently used by California Western School of Law including but not limited to the inventory set forth in Schedule B attached hereto and made a part hereof, free and clear of all encumbrances except any which are specifically set forth in Schedule C attached hereto and made a part hereof. (and USIU agree to accept)

3. California Western agrees to pay to USIU in full payment for the said properties described in paragraphs 1 and 2 hereinabove, the total sum of One million seven hundred and fifty thousand Dollars ($1,750,000) subject to the limitations and conditions and under the terms provided for hereinafter.

4. In partial payment of said purchase price California Western assumes and agrees to pay the following as of the closing date of this agreement:
a) The total sum of $480,000 to Connecticut Mutual Life Insurance Co.

$1,750,000 was the total price for land, building, library and all!

pursuant to that certain agreement and Deed of Trust executed by and between USIU and Connecticut Mutual under date of _____, 19__, as amended by _____, at the rate of $_____ month to which assumption Connecticut Mutual Life indicated its agreement

b) The total sum of $260,000 to Rubie Corporation pursuant to that certain agreement and Deed of Trust executed by and between USIU and Rubie Corporation under date of _____, 19__ as amended by _____, at the rate of $_____ per month, to which assumption Rubie Corporation has indicated its agreement by its execution of this agreement.

c) The total sum of $260,000 to Daley Corporation pursuant to that certain agreement and Deed of Trust executed by USIU and Daley Corporation under date of _____, 19__, as amended by _____, at the rate of _____, to which assumption Daley Corporation has indicated its agreement by its execution of this agreement.

No cash—only assumption of certain debts and a note

promptly paid first, out of any cash which may be paid or payable to USIU hereunder by others, or under the terms of the promissory note, Schedule D.

7. ~~It is agreed that~~ All tuition and other income of the said law school, from and after June 1, 1975, shall be paid to and be the property of California Western

8. From and after the closing date hereof, California Western agrees to assume the obligations of USIU as to all of the contracts described in Schedule F attached hereto and made a part hereof, provided however that nothing herein shall be deemed to relieve USIU of any of its past due or present obligations thereunder except as provided for herein.

9. In the event that the negotiations presently being conducted among Hastings College of Law, the George School of Law of University of the Pacific, California Western, and USIU

USIU remained liable for taxes and all unassumed debt.

(9) the set-off amounts set forth in Schedule E not yet paid or funded) toward the principal balance due on the promissory note in Schedule D, which said cash payment shall be credited against the last payments due thereunder.

11. The parties shall designate as of the closing date hereof, by written instrument of appointment, and maintain at all times, two persons as members of a Consortium Committee ~~hereby established~~ Said Committee shall set general Consortium policies and staff requirements, shall hire and discharge the consortium staff and shall maintain liaison with the respective parties. The compensation of the members of the Consortium Committee shall be the responsibility of the designating party. If the Consortium Committee is unable to resolve an issue, then the President of each party shall meet with the Consortium Committee as additional members thereof and the Committee thus

And of course a "consortium" was established!

UNITED STATES
INTERNATIONAL
UNIVERSITY

California Western Law School
350 Cedar Street
San Diego, California 92101
(714) 239-0391

Pro-forma
<u>Balance Sheet</u>

Assets

Cash	17,164.91
Building	1,000,000.00
Library, eqpt.etc.	750,000.00
	1,767,164.91

Liabilities

Salaries due	8,075.
Conn. Mutual	482,004.62
Cubic Corp.	242,070.72
D. Daley	269,786.90
Union Bank	400,000.00
USIU	356,137.76
	1,758,075.00
Net	9,089.91

SCHOOL OF LAW

Initial pro forma balance sheet of new corporation

Chapter X

Newly Independent Law School

To celebrate the culmination of the long months of work and worry and uncertainty, Toni and I invited the Castetters to dinner at Anthony's Star of the Sea on Harbor Drive overlooking San Diego Bay. We were all dressed in our finest and chatted in a cheerful mood as we ate and drank in one of the city's finest restaurants.

We toasted to being alive again and to the new free-standing law school. Then as the women talked, the Dean and I spoke of the future.

"I know you recognize the wonderful position you're in now. The first thing you'd better do is have a contract with the school as dean—and president. Probably three years.

"But, please remember you're now president of a corporation. All the staff and faculty are employees of the corporation, not yours. All the years I practiced, that had to be impressed on heads of closely-held businesses—overlooking it is easy and very dangerous. The temptation to use staff for private purposes is a temptation many people have a hard time overcoming." And it was a temptation with which Castetter may later have had difficulty.

Beginning to realize the enormous benefits to him from what had happened, it seems to me it was at that dinner that Castetter asked me what I wanted for my work and time, which he usually characterized as creative but really only nuts and bolts drafting and assistance in what he and Miller had accomplished.

"Only this, Dean. I want to go back to the quiet life of a law professor with your assurance that I will receive no less in pay than the highest paid faculty member and that you establish a Trial Practice Institute of which I'll be the director." He promptly assented, but no such Institute was ever established.

It was certainly at that dinner the dean dropped a real bombshell.

"I have something to tell you which you won't want to hear. Miller has submitted a bill for twenty-five thousand dollars, plus expenses."

"What in hell for?"

"Well, he really has done a lot, although that does seem a bit high."

"If he's billing for what I did it's not enough, but I really don't know what all he has done. Only you know that. Are you going to pay it?"

"Oh, I think we'll have to. We need his office now to keep on with the accounting and payroll work they're doing, and he is the school's lawyer."

It was evident to me that it would be paid, and by that time I realized that Castetter seemed really to believe that he and Miller had engineered what he perceived as the "separation" from USIU.

In early September, Judge Ault was elected the first Chairman of the Board of Trustees, and the early growing pains of the new institution began. Miller's fee was promptly paid, well before the delinquent faculty salaries and pension contributions were brought up to date, and a rather curious event occurred with respect to me.

Sometime in 1975, Castetter had hired Jack Reynolds, a tall, remarkably handsome mustachioed man, a former magazine publisher. He was apparently to do public relations, student recruiting and fund-raising, although actually he had become an able assistant to the dean in many matters. Jack came to me and told me that the dean or Miller wanted to give me a pen set for what I'd done in connection with the "separation." He said that he had told them he thought a pen set would be tacky and that he thought I'd much prefer a picture which I could pick out. He said they'd agreed, and that I should select something for $500, and he would have a little brass plaque made to put on it.

The picture I selected was a signed color serigraph, *Red Images,* of Victor Vasarely. It hangs in our home among our collection of original graphics. There is indeed a brass plaque which Reynolds had made for me to attach to the glass, with the inscription: "To Professor George N. Gafford in deep appreciation of your services in the founding of our new school. The Trustees of the California Western School of Law. September 3rd, 1975."

The plaque and Reynold's words have tarnished, but the sentiment expressed is treasured, although I'm afraid it does remind me of those newspaper articles which had so upset me. Regardless of my feelings, the big picture was that there was now every chance that the law school would survive and regain good standing with the American Bar Association and untainted membership in the Association of American Law Schools. We could all continue teaching, help improve a fully accredited independent law school, and enjoy living in San Diego.

In the spring of 1975, in the midst of all the school's problems, the existence of a national patent law moot court competition came to my attention. Although I knew little or nothing about patent law and the law school offered no major course in it, I was intrigued. It seemed to me that appellate argument was appellate argument, regardless of the subject matter. Fortunately, I was able to recruit two very excellent students to tackle the problem. Tom Koester was a tall man with a red mustache and a deep resonant voice, and Jeff Lewin, smaller and with a softer voice, was one of the brightest and most articulate men in his class.

When they first came to the house for a practice session, Toni asked Koester whether he sang professionally—so strong and distinctive was his speaking voice. Both men worked diligently at learning enough patent law to argue the problem, and practiced endlessly to perfect their presentations and answers to questions. The results were most gratifying—they not only won the regional competition but prevailed in the finals in Washington, bringing to the relatively young and very troubled school the recognition of its third national competition championship.

But there was still a great deal to be done and there were many problems to be solved before all would be well. California Western was still very far from being a truly first rate law school, and it still had its accreditation problems. Fortunately, after the closing of the sale and consortium agreement the new school, with its strange heritage and brave rebirth, inaugurated many years of steady and remarkable improvement through the efforts and wisdom of a great many people.

The first months were both frantic and chaotic. At the request of the faculty, one of the first acts of the new Board of Trustees was to grant tenure to all those faculty members who had had tenure under USIU. A committee of the tenured faculty was then formed, named the Faculty Executive Committee (FEC), with senior faculty member Bob Meiners as its first chairman. That committee met weekly for many long hours trying to establish the framework under which the newly autonomous school would operate. It met without the presence or participation of the dean. One of its purposes was for the first time to write the rules in accordance with the requirements of the American Bar Association and the Association of American Law Schools for faculty governance of law schools, which meant substantially limiting the power of the dean.

Careful rules were drawn for operating procedures completely different from those which obtained while the law school was a part of USIU. The rights and obligations of the faculty were defined, the procedures for hiring, tenure, sabbaticals and termination of dean and faculty were delineated to conform with the thoughts and desires of the tenured faculty and of the ABA and AALS.

The very well-credentialed Barbara Gamer (later a Superior Court judge) had already joined the faculty as the first woman faculty member since the librarian during the earliest years on Point Loma, along with Marcus Grantham, a former British barrister. They both added a great deal to the faculty, Gamer with her scholarship and gracious charm, and Grantham with his broad knowledge and wit—and particularly his admirable English accent!

After having won the hearts of faculty and students alike and contributing immensely to the school's international law and oral advocacy programs, Grantham suffered an untimely death of complications from relatively minor surgery. Mark Dennis, the gifted student who had designed the small stained glass window in the Moot Court, painted a colorful portrait of him which hangs in the school.

Dennis also played an important role in another daunting task, but one which I for one greatly enjoyed—establishing the flavor and identity of the newly independent school. Not only had we had the opportunity of creating the independence of the new school, but we now had the pleasure of building its individual substance, character and color!

We had to design a school seal, choose school colors, draw a school logo, and find unique and distinctive trademarks in both appearance and programs to identify the school and set it apart. What a thrill and challenge it was actually to be a part of making California Western now into a distinctive institution, an independent law school.

Dennis was called upon again to lend his artistic talents to the effort. A committee of Barbara Costley, Professors Culp and Gamer, and student Joel Junker was formed. After many suggestions and efforts, Dennis designed a circular school seal with an open book at the top, a hand and forearm holding the scale of justice, with the name of the school around the edge. My predilection for Latin was satisfied by having small banners on each side of the seal, with the word *Jus* in one and *Lex* in the other.

In later years the banners were somehow changed. Both Latin words now appear on the left banner and on the other one there now appears: "Est. 1924". (It will be recalled that 1924 was the date of incorporation of San Diego Chiropractic College, the corporate entity bought for use by Leland Stanford's new law school, with the name changed to Balboa Graduate University in 1933. The corporate name was again changed to Balboa University in 1950, then to California Western University of San Diego in 1952. The USIU corporation was merged into it and its name changed to United States International

University in 1967. Finally the law school assets were sold to the new corporation named California Western School of Law in 1975.)

The colors chosen for the school were lavender and gold, and a banner was designed in those colors to be carried at the head of the academic procession at each commencement. About that time Brad Phillips, a student who had been in the Alaskan legislature, was having a cruise ship built for cruising in Alaskan waters. He had found some excellent wood carvers in El Cajon east of San Diego to carve great painted wooden emblems to be installed on the sides of the new ship's bridge. When I saw their remarkable work, I took a drawing of our new school emblem and had them carve and paint two large wooden emblems for the school. One was placed behind the bench in the Moot Court and the other one on a movable podium.

Having been impressed with the artistry and skill of both Dennis and Barrett in making the little Moot Court window, Toni and I talked with them at length about designing and fashioning a stained glass window which might well become a logo of the law school. The large window at the head of the broad stairway leading up from the lobby was an ugly factory-type window made of a metal frame with chicken wire embedded in cloudy glass—hardly appropriate for so prominent a place in the law school. That was the window we hoped to disguise.

Ultimately there resulted exactly the drawing we envisioned, and Barrett was able to adapt Dennis' work into something that could be executed in glass and lead. Toni and I had the window made, framed in wood and installed as a gift to the law school in memory of our daughter Diane. The window is illuminated from behind by fluorescent lights. A red-robed judge on the right, the blindfolded, blue-robed lady of justice with her sword on the left, the newly-created emblem of the law school in the center, with the law school's facade below, the window is indeed often used as a logo of the school.

Amidst the tensions and turmoil of those infant years in the life of the new entity, much was accomplished and slowly the school, weaned from its mother, began to crawl and finally walk on its own.

During the first harried weeks, while the FEC was drawing the blue-prints for the new structure and before a proper business office could be established, the financial affairs were handled through Ralph Miller's office. Although Castetter had earlier been very much Miller's champion, as time went on that relationship began to cool.

Whether it was because Miller seemed to be acquiring too great an influence over the school's operations or faculty complaints he had delayed payment of their delinquent salaries, his participation diminished. Soon a business manager was hired and the school operated its own financial affairs. Ralph Miller's contribution had been substantial, and he has remained a friend of the school, even providing large student awards annually for excellence in tax law courses.

One of the first and most important immediate objectives of the new school was to overcome the accreditation difficulties which had resulted primarily from the financial limitations of the university. Within a few months after the agreement of purchase and sale there was to be an on-site inspection by the ABA and AALS, and it would fall to the faculty to prepare what was bound to be a most difficult self-evaluation. It would have to skate on the thin ice of being a law school overcoming the problems and being completely independent of the "bad" university but at the same time not being a new law school requiring first-time accreditation.

Even before the ABA inspection, the HEW representative had called a meeting to discuss the problems of the coming year and re-ports he had received of the separation of the law school from USIU. I was asked to attend, and Bill Rust's words ("No one knows what a consortium is") came back to me the moment the meeting began.

"First of all, let's discuss the application of the law school for accreditation by HEW."

"Oh, no", I said. "We're in a consortium with the university—there's no need to change a thing."

"Oh, yes! A consortium, h-um-m, Oh, yes. Well, how many eligible students do you expect this semester?"

Not a question about what the consortium was, what was meant by a consortium, or another word about it. We were home free with the GI Bill!

Would the rehabilitation with the ABA and the AALS had been as simple. In anticipation of the December, 1975, on-site inspection, the faculty was called upon to prepare the dreaded Faculty Self Study to present to the inspection team. That study, bearing the new school seal, provided a short history, the enrollment growth figures, the names of the part-time faculty and profiles of the full-time faculty (by then numbering fourteen), and descriptions of the curriculum and extra-curricular activities. There was also a listing of the interschool competitive victories, including the two best memorials and the two best oralists in the United States international moot court competitions, the two national client counseling championships, the national patent moot court championship, and the several appellate moot court and international moot court regional championships. The self study described the very successful law review and international law journal as well as the school's growing clinical program.

After describing the continuing efforts at achieving full faculty governance to comply with ABA-AALS guidelines, perhaps the most difficult part of the report covered the growing financial stability of the independent school. Since it was less than six months after the purchase of the school from USIU, the inspection team was especially concerned as to whether the school could survive the financial woes which had been the cause of the earlier problems leading to the threat of disaccreditation. Much was made of the fact that as an independent school California Western did not have a university to look to for financial support.

It was by the happiest of coincidences that we were able to attach to the documents given to the inspection team a lead article from the Wall Street Journal showing the many complaints of law schools whose parent universities were taking away as much as 50% of their tuition revenue—whereas California Western could retain all of its tuition revenue!

There followed trips by Castetter, Meiners, Ault, Culp, Galinson, Lay, Leahy and Howard Smith, the business manager, to ABA and AALS committee meetings, and a trip by Castetter and me to HEW. Full membership in the Association of American Law Schools was reinstated in November, 1976, and the "show cause" order of the American Bar Association was withdrawn and full accreditation reinstated in February, 1977. Ultimately the HEW interest in the building was transferred from USIU to Calfornia Western—to expire in May, 1990. After the "consortium" was later terminated pursuant to the terms of the original agreement, California Western was truly on its own and free of every cloud but one.

Only the IRS lien remained, and later in 1977 through a successful negotiation by Bob Fredrick, the former student and national Client Counseling champion, later a professor, that was removed. It was satisfied by a joint payment from USIU and California Western, the latter being credited against the original note to USIU.

And with survival assured, the law school was gradually consolidating its position. Professor Carroll Moreland, formerly Law Librarian at the University of Pennsylvania law school, was an outstanding addition to the faculty to organize the expanding law library as needed to meet accreditation standards.

Under the newly-adopted faculty governance procedures, during the academic year 1975-76, the Recruitment Committee interviewed approximately fifty candidates and considered many more applications. Arthur Campbell, John DeBarr, Bob Fredrick, Gerald Lopez, Wayne Westling and Richard Young were added to the faculty. All were well credentialed. Campbell had been a boxer at Harvard, had been an Assistant United States Attorney and private practitioner and done extensive teaching.

DeBarr was a highly-decorated retired Brigadier-General and had been Director of the Judge Advocate Division of the Marine Corps. Lopez was a bright, bearded young teacher, graduate of U.S.C. and Harvard Law School and a former U.S. District Judge clerk. Westling had been a Deputy District Attorney and had taught at the Universities of Sydney and of Oregon. Young had been in active practice for many years, and was an expert in Native American law, having served as tribal counsel and as director of the Native American Legal Defense Fund.

Gradually, as *Commentary*, the student newspaper reported, stability was returning to the school. Whereas it had been said that rules requiring the faculty to turn in grades within a certain time had been difficult to enforce when their salaries were not paid on time, new rules were now to be enforced requiring that exams be graded within 45 days for first year and 30 days for upper classes.

The student Law Revue was becoming a very sophisticated show, with a top magician like Scott Farr, the "Great Scott," and talented musicians like Steve Muni. The Clinical Board sponsored a mock trial for high school students in the Moot Courtroom, the Student Bar Association sponsored a golf tournament, and an article in *Commentary* urged that students should work and study as lawyers without becoming amoral in the process.

Much was said and written in the school about the need for more women in the law. In 1975, 16% of the student body were women, and the percentage rose steadily every year thereafter. One of the younger faculty members confided to me that although it was generally concealed from a senior member like me, many unmarried students were living together. Before long even we were allowed to know! By the same token, at first talk about homosexuality and gay rights was surreptitious, but it was soon quite frank and open, concerning both students and faculty members.

A survey of 300 law firms published by the *Harvard Law Record* indicated that 1975 law graduates started at an average salary of $15,000. Lawyers' billing rates had increased one or two dollars an hour to an average of $55 in California, $50 in Florida, and $42 in Ohio and the Southwest. And from the case of *Marvin v. Marvin*, the new word "palimony" was added to the legal lexicon.

In the 1976-77 academic year, the Faculty Recruitment Committee held some forty interviews. Richard Brown, a graduate of Princeton and Harvard Law School who had practiced law in New Orleans and was an experienced teacher, and Louis Friedman, a promising novice, were added to the faculty.

During the 1977-78 academic year, with the approval of two sabbatical leaves, the retirement of Carroll Moreland and the termination of another faculty member (for untoward speech and actions which would now be deemed sexual harassment), five new faculty members were added. They were Chin Kim, the new Law Librarian, Penn Lerblance, William Lynch, Michael O'Keefe and Katharine Rosenberry.

Chin Kim held degrees from Korea, Yale and George Washington Universities, and had been a faculty member at the Universities of Paris, Seoul, and Illinois. Penn Lerblance had been Assistant Attorney General of Oklahoma, Referee with the Court of Criminal Appeals, and a professor at Oklahoma City law school. Bill Lynch was a graduate of Boston College and Law School and had been a Navy Captain and Judge Advocate for more than twenty years.

Mike O'Keefe had practiced for many years as a Certified Public Accountant, had taught at both Willamette and the University of Washington, been Associate Dean and Acting Dean of Catholic University of America law school, and was a highly regarded expert in tax law. Katharine Rosenberry held degrees from Northwestern and Illinois Universities and the University of San Diego, had practiced some and was a most promising young teacher.

New offices were constructed for the Law Review at the east end of the library and Bob Fredrick became Assistant Dean. In a move to revive the Law Students' Civil Rights Research Council, an outgrowth of the activist sixties, it was renamed the New Law Coalition, and its members given an office on the law building's fourth floor. Classical music programs were held in the Faculty-Student Lounge on the third floor, and the Student Bar Association arranged for a speakers' program to provide diversion for the students.

There were the usual efforts by the SBA to obtain greater participation by students in the faculty governance of the law school, resulting in some committee participation being granted, some denied. Nevertheless, the general tenor of the relationships between the students and the faculty and administration had become cordial and constructive—in stark contrast to the confrontations and the bitterness of the two years between the move to Cedar Street and the school's purchase from USIU.

In 1979, Marilyn Ireland, former Associate Dean and member of the faculty of Washington University, joined the faculty. Scott Ehrlich, with a J.D. from New York University and an LL.M. from Harvard, and Jan Stiglitz, who also held an LL.M. from Harvard and had been an Assistant Attorney General in New York, became faculty members in the spring of 1980. Peter Gross, a graduate of Harvard College and Law School, also was added to the faculty to head an innovative and ambitious legal skills program. With this group the core faculty had been established at about twenty-five full-time members. Adding a few excellent new professors and losing some, it remained at around that number for several years.

But to back track a bit. Coincident with the independent law school's early growing pains, I had been exposed to an internal glimpse of USIU which portrays another facet of the law school's heritage. Shortly after the closing of the law school purchase agreement in August of 1975, Dr. Rust invited me to his office.

"George, now that together we've saved the law school, I'd like to have you work for the university. I need you to help me. I'm sure you would enjoy it, and we want your talents and experience.

"I'd like you to be a vice president of the university. I'm sure our financial troubles will soon be over, and I could pay you a lot more than you're making at the law school. Bob Dunn is now the vice president, as you know, but I'm satisfied that we need two vice presidents."

"Thank you very much, Bill, but I'm happy to go back to being a full-time law teacher. I left the law practice in part to get away from its stress and strain—and I don't want to get back into it."

"I wish you'd think it over. You could accomplish a great deal more here than you can teaching."

"No. I've reveled in doing the job we did, and I felt the juices really flow. I'm happier than you can imagine with the results, but this is it."

"You really should give it more thought. Talk to your wife about it."

"I'll talk to her, but I have no doubt the answer will be 'thank you, but no'."

"Well, in the meantime, with Bob away in Kenya, would you come out here part-time, use his office and give me the help I need while he's away?"

"If I can be of some help on a temporary basis, that might make sense. How much time would you have in mind?"

"Could you make two or three hours in the afternoon, twice or maybe three times a week? At say three hundred dollars a week for now—starting tomorrow?"

So it was that I spent several months in the administration building of USIU on the Elliott campus. Situated in Bob Dunn's office next to Dr. Rust's, my position was untitled, but it soon became evident that both my authority and responsibility were those of a vice president. In the anteroom in front of the two offices sat Dr. Rust's secretary, June Riddle, and Dunn's secretary, Lorraine Terp, who became mine temporarily. Rust and I were only a few feet apart, able easily to walk into each other's offices—which he did far more often than I.

The matters that I was called upon to handle were varied and interesting. One of the first and most difficult arose from the same problem as had plagued the law school—the university's faculty salaries were in arrears, and the unrest was growing daily. Following long discussions and careful negotiations, we arrived at a conclusion which was satisfactory to the faculty and staff and feasible for the university.

Assisted by outside counsel, I prepared documentation which provided for notes to be issued by the university to its faculty and staff covering all salary and pension delinquencies, with interest and principal payable quarterly over a period of five years. From the sale of the Mexico campus (then in escrow) there would be assigned $200,000 to a corporate trustee, plus $150,000 of current university receivables, $50,000 of the tuition to be received in December, 1975, and $50,000 of the tuition to be received in January, 1976. As security, the trustee was given a first lien on the books, catalogues, periodicals and other printed materials constituting the University Library.

The corporate trustee was to issue trust certificates to the employees evidencing their rights as beneficiaries under the trust agreement and the security agreement, and the employees were in return to give the university full releases of all back salary and TIAA/CREF (pension) obligations prior to January 15, 1976. There was probably no more precedent for that arrangement than there had been for the purchase of the law school, but a crisis was averted.

The many other matters which were handed me provided an excellent insight into the myriad problems of a university, especially of one in a precarious financial position. Shortly after the sale of the Mexican campus, the campus in Colorado was sold, with details flowing over to us at the Elliott campus.

There were several lawsuits, some by students, which were often frivolous, and others which were more serious. One involved a business hired to do student recruiting, which was accused of being incompetent and fraudulent, another involved a promised philanthropic contribution from the discoverer of a wrecked treasure-carrying vessel in the Caribbean.

The issue with the treasure ship was far exceeded by another problem involving gold with which I was not involved, but about which I learned while working in the executive offices.

It seems that there was a Canadian missionary in Kenya named Dean Remple. Apparently more of an adventurer and confidence man than a man of God, Remple approached Warren Hamilton, the provost of the USIU campus in Nairobi with a sure-fire scheme to untold riches. He said that he knew where large caches of gold, stolen by Idi Amin from his own people and others, were secretly stored for the easy taking in several small homes in neighboring Uganda (where Amin was president from 1971-1979).

The justification was that since the gold had been stolen and did not rightly belong to Amin, it would not be improper to truck it out of Uganda to be used in God's work—and other proper but far less charitable uses. It was reported that Hamilton and others had advanced some of their own funds in furtherance of the project, but that Remple had found it necessary to provide a sizeable sum as security to show the good faith of the investors before the disclosure of the exact location of the gold, hiring of the trucks and the actual transportation of the gold could begin. (How could any educated adult have been deluded by such a well-worn con?)

Remple was so convincing that Hamilton—having the apparent authority—committed USIU to a $500,000 letter of credit at the Commercial Bank of Africa. The letter of credit was not to be used, but only shown as evidence of good faith. Instead, the letter of credit obviously was called upon, and USIU suffered an unrecoverable loss of one-half million dollars.

By the late fall of 1976, the law school back salaries having been brought up to date and the school's operations approaching normal, it was time to give thought to taking the sabbatical leave to which I was entitled—the value of all faculty sabbatical accruals having been included in the financial computations of the law school purchase. My wife and I began to make plans for what would be the dream of a lifetime: six months in Europe.

My scholarly project was to be a comparison study of the legal ethics of several European countries with the United States, as well as their views regarding and possible use of contingent fee lawsuits. I wrote to lawyers in this country and abroad for relationships which would provide me with the names of lawyers and law teachers whom I could interview.

When the problem of transportation during such a long European stay arose, Bill Rust made the suggestion to me that we buy a Volkswagen diesel, which he had heard was available in Germany.

"That would be really cheap and easy transportation while you're there, and you could probably sell it for as much or more than you paid for it. And while you're over there, be sure to visit our campus at Evian. I'll arrange for our director there to make you both welcome and you could stay there if you like."

Rust's suggestion about a diesel made sense, and we discovered we could arrange for the purchase of the new 5-cylinder Mercedes diesel, to be delivered in Sindelfingen, outside Strasbourg, and ship it back to the United States after our sojourn in Europe, probably to be sold at a profit. And that is what we determined to do.

All the financial matters which had to be handled while we were gone, as well as the many other details which a long stay away from home entailed were left in the capable hands of Phil Sbarbaro[31], a former student who had become a close friend.

Early in the trip we drove along the beautiful southern shore of Lake Geneva to Evian-les-Bains. After Dr. Rust had dispatched Bob Dunn to investigate appropriate places for a USIU branch in France or Switzerland, Dunn had been steered to Evian, once a posh French resort. There he met with Mayor Foch, a nephew and the last male of the line of the great French *marechal*. The mayor had pointed out several formerly luxurious resorts, and had helped greatly in obtaining the necessary permits for a school.

Under severe financial pressure, the hotel Dr. Rust had unfortunately chosen to lease was in serious disrepair, but with a priceless view overlooking the lake. With some difficulty Toni and I found that French "campus"—a most disillusioning sight. With its beautiful view, but in utter disrepair, it looked especially forlorn on a drab winter day. We saw a total of ten or fifteen students in the cold and dark corridors, then met with Bill Clarke, the director.

He was charming and buoyant, apparently fluent in both English and French, and urged us to spend the night with them, which we declined. We did enjoy speaking with him and some of the students,

---

[31] Phil had been one of the first winners of the Diane Ethics Scholarship. A cash award we have given at both California Western and Case Western Reserve law schools, it is presented to the graduating student "who has demonstrated throughout law school, in academic, professional and extracurricular activities, the best understanding and high ideals of the legal profession."

learned there were only a very few altogether, and avoided any com-ments about the terrible facility. How many other teachers there were, if any, was not mentioned, but strange as it seemed to us, both the director and the students were apparently happy and more than satisfied with the school and their experience.

Chapter XI

Further Growing Pains and a New Dean

The developments during the first years of the law school as an independent institution were as interesting as the gradual changes in its dean. From being simply the dean he became dean and president, and then the Chief Executive Officer. From the black banlon shirts and bolo ties of Point Loma came elegant suits—and added weight. From a clean shaven face came a full beard, and from a bare head came an omnipresent cap—and the conservative gray Thunderbird became a Corvette with a distinctive license plate: "evry day."

Approval having been received of the transfer of the federal interest in the law school building from USIU to California Western, it was no longer a concern. Likewise, the nominal "Academic Consortium" had served its purpose. Accordingly, Dr. Rust had been notified in the fall of 1976 that California Western waived its option to rescind the June 8, 1975, purchase agreement because of the federal interest. In early 1977, I drew an agreement executed by the parties to conclude all unresolved matters resulting from that original contract.

The principal balance of the promissory note to the university as the result of payments and set-offs was agreed to be corrected to be only $90,000, reduced by the $50,000 then paid by California Western along with the payment by USIU which removed the IRS lien on the building. The balance of $40,000 was to be paid in monthly payments of $444.10 beginning in January 1978, with interest at 6%. The parties further mutually agreed to withdraw from the Academic Consortium, and in essence, but for the small note payments, released each other from further obligations.

The divorce from USIU was a *fait accompli*, any risks of liens had been removed, and California Western School of Law was truly and completely independent and on its own.

As the debt was being paid off, and as the student body and the budget grew larger, with the addition of more faculty came also additional administrative personnel. First there was a business manager, then an independent auditing firm, then a business office, an associate dean and soon a vice dean, as well as one and then a second assistant dean. For a very short time there was even a professional counselor to the students.

There was a procession of people during the first years in the effort to build an organization not only for the daily operation of the law school but also to try to begin true placement efforts and the establishment of alumni support and fund-raising. Castetter and his wife made numerous trips, often to Hawaii and other favorable locales, to meet with alumni. He had a particular rapport and was most highly regarded by many of the graduates with whom he had been close during the early years when the school was on Point Loma and small. Jack Reynolds, named Director of Development, also traveled a great deal in the fund-raising effort, although the results in real dollars from either of their efforts were relatively small.

At the same time, Castetter slowly was able to hand-pick new members to the Board of Trustees, some who were possibly helpful for prestige in the accreditation problems, but not any members who would provide real momentum to fund-raising. In fact Castetter was so reticent in that regard that he felt he had to assure those he sought for the Board that no calls would be made upon them for financial support. As a result, the faculty gradually came to resent and question the validity and desirability of such a board. It was looked upon as a group of people chosen by and subject to the direction of the dean, who contributed little or nothing to the school or its welfare and yet had control over the income and careers of the faculty whose very lives were dependent on the law school.

Despite the faculty's having gained far greater governance through the new operating procedures than had ever existed while the school was still part of USIU, there was growing dissatisfaction with the situation vis-a-vis the dean and "his" Board of Trustees. While that was understandable, unfortunately many on the faculty failed to appreciate at all the time and interest that many of the board members did give to the school without reward. Judge Ault as the first board chairman had given an enormous amount of his time and wisdom, and contributed greatly in the regaining of unblemished accreditation. Likewise Judge Levenson contributed substantially and served faithfully as vice-chairman until his early death.

Alec Cory, a prominent San Diego attorney who followed Ault as chairman, was an excellent moderating influence on the infant corporation, as was Judge Frank Orfield who next served as chairman. Most of the board members during the first few years, however, served for relatively short periods, pretty much followed Castetter's lead, and made limited individual contributions of importance to the success of the new institution.

Among the longest serving of the early board members were Judge Robert Kingsley, an appellate judge from Los Angeles and a former dean of USC law school, who lent dignity and experience to the board, as did Sam Thurman, dean emeritus of the University of Utah law school, and Manfred Schrupp, dean emeritus of the School of Education of San Diego State University. Jim Gillean, a retired banker, acted as treasurer of the corporation and gave many hours of productive time to the school.

Following in the footsteps of Dr. Rust, who as a university president was the consummate purchaser of real estate, the Board in late 1977 authorized the purchase of a two-storey house on First Avenue, about six blocks away from the law school. The house had five bedrooms available for double occupancy by students, and their rental provided for the mortgage payments and upkeep of the house. After a few years of such operation as a student dormitory, however, the house was sold.

Desired first to provide much needed parking, the land purchase of important and lasting consequence was the property on Cedar Street across from the law school between Second and Third Avenues. Castetter with great foresight (actually first contemplating a high-rise office building) strongly believed in the desirability of its acquisition. In April, 1978, the school obtained a six-month option for $1000 to purchase the property for $250,000. The Board of Trustees subsequently authorized the purchase, and the property was used for faculty and staff parking for several years. Much later it was that acquisition which made possible the construction of the law school's administration building, the second of its eventual three-building campus at the intersection of Cedar Street and Third Avenue.

The third real estate transaction was the purchase of an old former small hotel on Second Avenue contiguous to the parking lot property, also to be used as a student dormitory. It was sold after troublesome operating problems and insufficient student demand.

It was in 1979 that the Shah of Iran was forced into exile, replaced by the Ayatollah Khomeini, and nearly 100 Americans were taken hostage. Also in that year President Carter, Israeli Premier Manachem Begin and Egyptian President Anwar Sadat reached the Camp David Accord. Margaret Thatcher became Conservative Prime Minister of Great Britiain and Mother Teresa won the Nobel Peace Prize. Death came to early film star Mary Pickford and to actor John Wayne, known as the "Duke." Karen Silkwood was posthumously awarded $10,500,000 damages for negligent exposure to atomic contamination.

By 1979, Dennis Avery, an alumnus, had been added as Assistant Dean for Placement and Alumni Relations, there was a more experienced Business Manager with an assistant and an accountant, a Financial Aid Director and two assistants, an admissions secretary, placement assistant, and even three faculty secretaries.

Also in that year California Western's Italian Renaissance building, as a structure of historical and artistic significance, and a nostalgic reminder of years of grandeur, was designated a "Historical Landmark".

Among the additions to the faculty was an attractive and very promising young man with an excellent academic background whose athletic and outdoor life-style and attitudes related unusually well to the students. Unfortunately he became enamored of the comely receptionist-telephone operator and was seen leaning over the counter in conversation with her by the hour, greatly limiting his time for class preparation and student counseling. When his probationary contract was not renewed, we learned that the young lady accompanied him to his next post.

It was around that same time that there were two examples of the impact of faculty governance with which I did not agree—whether from principle or my feeling toward the two individuals involved. Bob Fredrick had had a successful career as a real estate developer before he entered law school and although long out of college he had been a good student in law school. He had also been one of the two members of the team which won the Regional and then the National Client Counseling Competition, and successfully practiced law in San Diego for several years before he was asked to join the law school faculty.

When he was considered for tenure, the principle objection raised by his colleagues was insufficient academic credentials. It was suggested that if he would pursue a graduate degree it would then be appropriate that he be awarded tenure.

John DeBarr had had a 34-year military career and had been an outstanding Brigadier General in the United States Marine Corps with wide experience. He had served in legal positions for 26 of his years in the service, and was the Director of the Judge Advocate Division during his last three years.

When DeBarr was being considered for tenure, some allegations about his being less than brilliant as a teacher were made as they had been with Fredrick, although both were highly regarded by their students. And in DeBarr's case much was made of the assertions that his legal writings had not been truly scholarly but were of a more populist nature.

Actually, what both cases revealed to me was that there was an underlying reason, other than the apparent ones given, for the refusal to grant tenure to those two outstanding men. From my perspective it was a reason which rightly or wrongly seems to permeate academe, certainly law faculties. Many seem to place far greater emphasis and weight on academic distinction than worldly success. Given the same writings, the same teaching abilities and the same participation in law school and community affairs, other faculty members with prestigious academic credentials would I believe have been granted tenure. On the other hand, this observation may really be but a part of the ongoing dichotomy: is law school a graduate school in the discipline of the law or a professional school training students to become lawyers? Here again I see the need for compromise. It must be both, and for that reason requires teachers with varied talents and experience.

Chin Kim, the director of the law school library, demonstrated during his long tenure a remarkable combination of scholar and practical administrator. He single-handedly established and operated a program leading to the degree of Master of Comparative Law. To that program he attracted numerous graduate students, including many Korean judges and others, managed the library superbly, and at the same time wrote and published extensively. It was under Kim that the library became a first-rate law school library, properly staffed and organized.

After two or three years of effort to add student perspective to the law school Board of Trustees, it was finally persuaded to elect each year a former student, one year after graduation, as a member of the board for just one year. Likewise, both student and faculty representatives were invited to attend board meetings, which resulted in allaying much of their suspicion and reducing their criticism of the board.

Nevertheless, although the change in student attitudes from the last two years of the school's having been a part of USIU to the early years of its independence was dramatic, some sense of dissatisfaction remained. The school newspaper reported mostly the news and positive achievements, but there still were many complaints. There were loud concerns over the lower California bar exam passage rates of the graduates, and calls for faculty evaluations by the students—which were instituted.

With constant improvement of the physical facilities many of the former complaints of both the students and faculty were gradually appeased and actually with those improvements a greater *esprit de corps* achieved. Air conditioning and public address systems were improved and added, halls were carpeted, classrooms and faculty offices upgraded, the elevator renovated, tiered seating and permanent desks installed in the Moot Courtroom, and accommodation of handicapped persons accomplished. Projection screens and improved chalk boards, as well as substantial audio-visual equipment were added, and a mini-computer purchased.

The students actively sought representation on all faculty committees, and to some they were invited. There was more active participation in the Law Review and the International Law Journal and the many professional activities open to the students. Students vied to become members of the Advocacy Honors Board (I'd changed its name from Moot Court Board) and the Client Counseling Board. The Law Revue and the Barristers' Ball became major annual events. There were athletic competitions, the Student Bar Association and the Honor Court operated smoothly, food was served in the fourth floor student lounge, *Commentary* was a regularly published bi-weekly—California Western was beginning to come of age as a law school.

But there were concerns, shared by some of the faculty, over the school's name. There was an unaccredited law school, and solely a law school, improperly named the Western State *University* College of Law with a sizeable branch in San Diego. It was both disconcerting and somewhat demeaning to both students and faculty when others confused their attendance or teaching at California Western School of Law with an unaccredited night school.

Also there was a proprietary correspondence school in southern California which advertised widely, especially in airline publications, calling itself California Western University. The owners apparently thought they were free to do so in the belief that the name California Western University had been given up when it was changed to USIU. Although they had disregarded a letter sent them by USIU ordering them to desist, no suit was filed by the university which was then in the midst of its financial throes.

Counsel for the newly-independent law school was instructed to pursue the matter. The chief problem legally was the delay in filing the lawsuit (known in the law as "laches"). The correspondence school claimed that relying on the fact that no suit had been filed, it had spent many thousands of dollars in advertising, brochures, stationery, forms etc. on the name.

Dean Castetter testified as to the harm done the law school and the extent of the confusion caused by the correspondence school's use of the name, and I testified that the name and its value had been included in the negotiations and the contract of purchase of the law school from the university. It was our good fortune that the judge who heard the case found the laches to be insufficient to prevent relief in this case and ordered the defendant to change its name, allowing it a period of eight months for the transition. The defendant's appeal to a higher court was unsuccessful, and its name was changed to California Coast University.

With the disposition of that name problem, gradually as the law school's own name and reputation improved, the concern about the confusion with Western State abated. More recently the concern has completely disappeared, since that school's name was changed to Thomas Jefferson.

However the faculty's concerns with the administration continued and grew, until a reorganization was urgently sought. Mike O'Keefe was named to chair a committee charged with such reorganization, and it then fell to him and me to persuade the dean of its desireability. The dean and the board acceded to the new plan which provided that Castetter would no longer be dean but as CEO be charged solely with the tasks of fund-raising and overseeing the fiscal affairs of the school. O'Keefe was to take over as Vice Dean, and a dean search committee was formed which entered promptly on its task.

By 1980 the full-time faculty had grown to twenty-seven, and a new dean had been found. It was indeed fortuitous for the law school that a man of remarkable achievements and experience became available to serve. Ernest C. Friesen was chosen by the faculty and appointed with the enthusiastic approval of the Board of Trustees. Friesen was an alumnus of Columbia University Law School and a Senior Fulbright Fellow, had been an Assistant Attorney General with the Department of Justice, Dean of the National Judicial College, a faculty member at several universities and most recently Dean of Whittier Law School.

That was the year Andrei Sakharov, Nobel-laureate physicist, was stripped of honors in the U.S.S.R. and sent into internal exile in Gorky, Ronald Reagan was elected 40th President of the United States and Republicans gained control of the Senate for the first time since 1964. An American airborne commando raid to rescue the hostages in Iran failed disastrously, and there were the widely-reported deaths of Jimmy Durante (the "schnoz"), film director Alfred Hitchcock, actor George Raft, and Marino Marini, the celebrated Italian sculptor and painter.

Dean Friesen was given a most difficult task which he performed admirably. His deanship was to be the transition between the long years of Castetter, both loved and derided, and the new direction in which the faculty hoped the law school was destined to travel. Castetter had seen the school through its early years, had successfully presided over its early "mom and pop" period through ABA accreditation and AALS membership, and valiantly weathered much of the USIU financial morass and the consequent accreditation difficulties.

He had long served the law school well and had made many difficult and excellent decisions, even as he was overwhelmed by the threat of the financial failure and demise of the school. He may well have been worn out and less than enthusiastic to manage a substantial enterprise at the same time as being a member of the Board of Trustees, working with a large and more independent faculty, and attempting the very new and difficult obligation of major fund-raising.

Unburdened by the past or by trustee or fund-raising problems, Dean Friesen brought in an entirely new and different management style. He did not believe that anyone should stay as dean of a new law school for more than four or five years, and he had left Whittier Law School because he felt he had guided it to national accreditation, served his purpose and run out of ideas. He looked upon California Western as a challenge, an institution in the stage of its development where it needed some innovative, creative work. He believed the school needed development in community relations, to be better known in its own community, and recognized nationally as a school with a good faculty and a strong program.

A polished and worldly man, Friesen had been the administrator of the federal court system under Chief Justice Earl Warren and then under Chief Justice Warren Burger. For four years he had been the director of the Institute of Court Management, which trained some 300 court administrators. Thereafter he had studied the English court system and written a book called *English Criminal Justice*, before becoming dean of Whittier. His vision for California Western was to see "…a strong sense of purpose in the faculty and a recognition of what they need to maintain this unique quality. It will be a dynamic, changing institution as the needs of the legal profession change."

Friesen's wide contacts and friendship with judges throughout the country provided California Western graduates far greater ability to secure court clerkships and gain other desirable entrées. From those friendships also came William A. Grimes, an outstanding Distinguished Visiting Professor, former Chief Justice of the Supreme Court of New Hampshire, and among numerous other accomplishments a charter faculty member of the National Judicial College.

During Friesen's tenure also were added numerous other faculty members in the long procession over the years, some who remained and many who moved on. Among them were Julius Cohen, William Beaney and Dale Vliet (Distinguished Visitors), Mary Cook, Stephen Dunbar, Elliott Hahn, Dirk Metzger (son of a Marine general), Janet Motley, Therese De Saint Phalle (related to the noted artist), Stephen Mayo, Robert Bohrer, John Noyes, Lloyd Cohen, Neil Gotanda, Janeen Kerper, Paul Savoy, Glenn Smith, and Ann Wheeler.

Penn Lerblance succeeded Mike O'Keefe as Vice Dean and an unusual and interesting man joined the faculty. Walter Barnett was a summa cum laude graduate of Yale, a Fulbright scholar, a Harlan Fiske Stone and Playboy Foundation fellow. He wrote a book on the life of Jesus, and then while earning his master's degree at Columbia School of Law he wrote a book on the unconstitutionality of repressive sex laws. He had also written a part of the Pornography Commission Report as well as a pamphlet for the Quakers (he was a recently converted Quaker) entitled *Homosexuality and the Bible*.

"To find out how the lowest part of our society lives", the recently divorced father had lived on "skid row" receiving $3 a week, plus his room and board, working for the Catholic Worker just before coming to teach at California Western. Within a very short time, however, Barnett asked to be released from his teaching contract, saying, "I don't like teaching law anymore. I just couldn't force myself to do it. I will just have to find another field."[32]

Under Dean Friesen law school events and proceedings, indeed the law school itself, changed. From the relatively folksy atmosphere fostered by the gregarious Castetter of the early years it became more orthodox, more restrained and more professional. Under Friesen also the very innovative trimester system was introduced, with California Western becoming one of only two accredited law schools in the country providing students the opportunity of entering school in

[32] Caifornia Western *Commentary*, October 13, 1981

January and, by attending school three semesters each year, completing the requirements and graduating in only two calendar years.

The very smart and attractive Mary Jo Riley, with her strong Boston accent, became the new Placement Director and helped make that department more effective. The same autumn the school had enrolled, at sixty five, its oldest first-year law student. Sidney Warren held a Ph. D. in history and had retired after a distinguished 38-year career as a college professor. He had written five books, dozens of articles and encyclopedia entries, was a nationally recognized expert on the presidency and as such had been interviewed by Barbara Walters. Warren was one among many with previous careers who added enormously both to the student experience and to the pleasure of teaching. Both Castetter and Friesen, as well as many on the faculty, unlike at many law schools, believed that older students not only should be given the opportunity of becoming lawyers but also added a great deal to the education of their classmates. Business people, social workers, physicians, retired military officers, musicians, and accountants were among their many previous occupations.

For example, one of two physicians in his class, Dr. John Burroughs, formerly a thoracic surgeon and head of a heart team at UCLA hospital, became an outstanding member of one of my moot court competition entries. The greatest difficulty for the older and previously successful people was to revert to being students again, participate in student activities and concerns, and most of all to be respectful and attentive to professors much younger and with far less life experience.

Many physical changes and improvements were made during Friesen's tenure, some widely accepted, others greeted with less enthusiasm. The largest amphitheater classroom on the second floor was remodeled into two smaller classrooms and several faculty offices with outside windows on the perimeter of the building. Separate offices for the president and dean were provided, and numerous other structural and cosmetic improvements made throughout the building.

The school sought to maintain an enrollment of approximately 700 students, with an entering class of 250-300, plus the Master of Comparative Law program. The law school bulletin in the early eighties described a library of over 125,000 volumes (to reach more than 170,000 by the mid-eighties), an auditorium, audio-visual services, the Moot Courtroom, model attorney's office with one-way mirror and closed circuit TV. It described scholarly publications and professional activities of Law Review, International Law Journal, Institute for the Study of International Law, Advocacy Honors Board, Client Counseling Board, Clinical Education Board, and the Foreign Law Librarians Internship Program.

Activities were the Student Bar Association, Barrister's Ball, Canadian Student Bar Association, Honor Code, Phi Alpha Delta, Sigma Nu Phi and Phi Delta Phi legal fraternities, International Law Society, Cal Western Law Association for Women, Clinical Education Program, California Western Civil Liberties Association, California Western Student Trial Lawyers Chapter, Book Store, Minority Student Association, the *Commentary*, and California Western Theatrical Association—Law Revue.

There were five types of major financial aid programs administered by the school, as well as nine emergency revolving loan funds (four named in honor of Professors Burby, Culp, Chapin and Snedeker), plus six scholarship funds, part-time campus employment and several other types of educational aid opportunities.

What changes had been wrought since the Balboa night school, since the modest Point Loma beginnings, since the faculty increased to eight (all men) when I joined it, since the painful move and student struggles to help make the former Elks Hall and Performing Arts building livable for a law school, since the student tuition boycott, since the alleged 45,675 volume library and the staggering unpaid library bills and faculty salaries long overdue. And many dramatic changes were yet to come!

Chapter XII

Dreams of Merger and a Changing Board of Trustees

The faculty enthusiastically endorsed Ernie Friesen's reappointment by the Board of Trustees to a second three-year term as dean. Under him they had embarked upon true faculty governance. There was no area of the school's administration in which they were not involved. There were faculty committees for academic affairs, admissions, budget and finance, clinic, curriculum, facilities, faculty appointments, faculty development and performance, financial aid and awards, graduate studies, library, professional responsibility, research and writing, student affairs—in addition to the faculty executive committee!

The library budget was increased substantially, word processors and the first electronic legal research facilities were introduced, air-conditioning was installed in the Moot Court, and further physical improvements were made to the law school building. But there was still a growing undercurrent of faculty unrest. As early as January of 1981, minutes of a faculty meeting indicated that the faculty was seeking a voice in the selection of members of the Board of Trustees. By June of that year the faculty asked the Board to form a joint committee with the faculty for that purpose. Castetter, Schrupp and Gillean were appointed for the Board, while Friesen, Leahy and I served for the faculty, but it was some time before the kinds of changes desired were effected.

Nevertheless, in very many ways the six years that Friesen was dean of the law school were truly years of consolidation and growth. The school was settling in as a school which was seeking to become as secure and permanent as the stately building which housed it. Friesen and the faculty had made considerable strides toward increasing both its visibility and reputation, yet much still remained to be done.

It seemed to me that in the dichotomy between law school as a graduate school and as a professional school, my experience and inclination best suited me to the latter role. It was my strong belief that we were trying to educate students to become lawyers, and by trying to do that better than other schools we could best serve our students and also enhance the school's reputation. That was where my emphasis lay in both substantive courses and in trial practice and client counseling training.

For some years in teaching the Business Organizations course, I had developed a series of tasks for the students to perform that had nothing to do with casebook corporation law, which was the kind of law primarily involved in corporate litigation—and on the bar exam.

Just as Professor Jim Leahy had his students draw and probate wills, my students had first to draw up the Articles of Incorporation of a for-profit corporation, then of a not-for-profit corporation, and then of a professional corporation. Next they had to file those articles with the appropriate agency of their state. Then they had to organize the corporations with the necessary minutes of meetings, and next take the appropriate actions necessary for the sale of the securities of a for-profit corporation. There followed the minutes of all sorts of directors' and shareholders' authorizations and meetings, various sorts of corporate actions, cash and stock dividend declarations, stock splits, mergers and ultimately dissolutions.

Another example of that approach was in the course known as Remedies where I had the students actually prepare court decrees. The cases all involved various controversies in what is known as the law of equity, which concluded with the court's decision. In actual practice, after reaching its decision, the court normally orders that the prevailing party prepare the decree, which then must be submitted to the opposing party and the court. The preparation of that decree to conform to the court's ruling, different in each case, is the actual job of the lawyer.

These are but a few illustrations of the effort to teach the students to use the cases they studied in order to advise their clients how to avoid the controversies which precipitated the reported lawsuits, and how actually to perform the tasks of lawyers. Historically, the study of law has been to teach rules of law by the reading of appellate decisions. From such reading it seemed to me and others that too often the emphasis—and the lesson—was how best to win or defend against such a lawsuit. On the contrary, many law teachers now believe that they ought best be used to show how a client can be advised to avoid that sort of controversy, for that is by far the most constructive service an attorney can provide and is most often the problem facing the practicing attorney who is not a trial specialist.

Not considered by most law schools until the early 1970's, the rudiments of the techniques of client counseling were the stuff of the Client Counseling Board and both intraschool and interschool client counseling competitions which were established and fostered at California Western. Murray Galinson taught an innovative and popular course in Interviewing, Negotiating and Counseling, and other so-called practical courses had been added to the curriculum, such as Pre-trial Practice, Arbitration, Mediation, Appellate Advocacy, and even Practice Formation. Soon there became popular in many schools the enlargement of an old concept in new clothing called ADR, or Alternative Dispute Resolution, which gave more academic credibility to the study of arbitration, mediation and settlement.

When controversy cannot be avoided and a dispute cannot be solved by any other means, then of course the lawyer must know how actually to try the lawsuit, from beginning to end. Here again, most law schools were remarkably late and slow in their approach.

When I was in law school, trial practice was referred to as a "pedestrian talent to be learned after law school," and it was not until the nineteen sixties and seventies that it was even considered by most schools. At California Western, General Jim Snedeker began what was called Practice Court shortly after the dedication of the new law school building on Point Loma in 1963. Minutes of an early faculty meeting disclose that Judge Ault, who years later became the first Chairman of the Board of the newly-independent California Western, presided over the first student trial.

From the time of my arrival on Point Loma and then especially after the school moved to Cedar Street and its beautiful Moot Court, what came to be called Trial Practice became my bailiwick and my passion. There were few course models or examples to follow and little written on the subject, but lots of experimentation. While since time immemorial there had been interschool competitions in appellate moot court, there were at first no interschool competitions in jury trials. In more recent years, these competitions have proliferated.

At first we prepared skeleton fact situations which were given to teams of two students, one team designated as the plaintiff, the other as defendant. The students had to prepare the pleadings, motions and briefs, procure two witnesses for each side, and then at the end of the course, try the case to a jury of students before an actual San Diego judge. During the class sessions various invited members of the Bar and I addressed the students. One attorney would talk on such subjects as the preparation of a complaint, another on the answer, others on various motions and demurrers, opening statements, direct examination, cross-examination, proof of damages, objections, and final argument.

The willingness of the San Diego bar to give their time and talent in speaking to the students and in judging the trials was remarkable. Prominent plaintiffs' lawyers like Dave Casey and Red Boudreau and defense counsel like Bob Steiner and Gary Bailey were of enormous help.

Reading and correcting the written work, and embellishing the advice of the visiting attorneys was my task. The San Diego bench was remarkably cooperative, and there resulted a close acquaintance and association with them for me and for the school.

The students were thrilled to be able to appear before Federal judges like William Enright, Leland Nielsen and Gordon Thompson, Court of Appeal justices like Gerald Brown and Vincent Whelan. The Superior Court and Municipal Court judges willingly gave up long evenings to enrich the program and generously share their expertise. A few that I recall as being especially helpful and effective were William Yale (who later served the law school as a Trustee), Franklin Orfileld (later Board chairman), Jack Levitt, Joseph Kilgarif, James Focht, Gilbert Harelson, Bruce Iredale, Louis Welsh and Douglas Woodworth.

But that format needed to be improved, and a next step was the use of video cameras and critiques to help with the preparation of the students. It seemed most important that they be able to learn by doing and being critiqued in practice, and not having to wait until the actual trial. Later a model was found which became very successful. The class was limited to fifty, and divided into groups of ten with a separate instructor for each group, coached individually, in addition to the large class instruction.

Fortunately, we were able to induce unusually willing and experienced people to take on what to them was a labor of love. The first five men were retired Nevada Supreme Court Chief Justice David Zenoff, Superior Court Judges David Gill and William (Ted) Todd (later Justice of the Court of Appeal), and assistant U.S. Attorneys Raymond (Jerry) Coughlan and Robert Semmer. Judges Gill and Todd continued their participation for years and became bulwarks of the trial practice program.

In addition, as an experiment for two or three years I brought in Ronald Arden, a professional producer/ director/ actor, and professor at USIU's School for Performing Arts. Arden met with all the students in small groups and individually to help them with their speaking: voice control, elocution and body language. The experiment was well received and seemed to me to be of obvious help to many of the students, but ended when Arden's busy schedule made it impossible for him to continue.

With that caliber of instruction and lots of practice, and with the excellent training in evidence they had previously received from Ed Infante, a federal Magistrate and Professor Bill Lynch, former Navy Judge Advocate, both experienced litigators, they were well prepared. By the time of their actual trials at the end of the year most of the students demonstrated that they really knew the basics of trying a lawsuit. Often the judges would remark that they wished the attorneys appearing before them would be as polished and well prepared as the students.

The interschool competition teams which were developed from the trial practice program were a source of pleasure and pride to me and to the law school. California Western teams came to be regarded as the ones to beat. As they won successive regional championships, there was greater and greater interest among our students, which in turn produced continuously increasing participation and stronger competitive teams. Early among those was the team of Bruce Schechter and Tom Lotz , who were victorious in the regional competition at Brigham Young University, with the team of Doug Glauser and Dennis Amador doing almost as well, and the team of Robert Gaston, Margaret Lafko and Joyia Zapantis being victorious the very next year—California Western teams winning in three of the previous six years.

At the same time the law school's clinical program was making significant strides in becoming one of the students' favorite activities providing a service to the community as well as true hands-on experience for them. Peter Gross, an unusually innovative professor dedicated to finding better ways to teach writing skills and legal research to first year students teamed with Janet Motley, another gifted teacher, in creating outstanding programs for the school.

Also during Dean Friesen's tenure, Jim Leahy established and directed a Jurist in Residence program which was extremely successful and was often emulated by other schools. At the first such program, Supreme Court Justice William Rehnquist and Circuit Court of Appeals Judge Myron Bright spent a week at the school, both lecturing and speaking with the students on a variety of subjects and providing them with an insight into the workings of the federal District Courts, Circuit Courts and the Supreme Court. They were joined at various times by former New Hampshire Chief Justice Grimes of the faculty, as well as Judge Judith Keep, of the federal District Court in San Diego.

Occupying a great deal of attention in the early 1980's, and some dreaming also, were the efforts to accomplish a merger between California Western and the University of California at San Diego. Richard Atkinson, now the President of the University of California, but then the Chancellor of the San Diego campus, believed a law school was necessary to a great university. On more than one occasion he had indicated to me that a merger with California Western would provide the likeliest avenue for UCSD to achieve that goal. Committees were formed and meetings arranged among Castetter, Friesen, Assistant Chancellor Pat Ledden, Judge Orfield, Fred Schrupp, Sam Thurman, DeWitt Higgs, and former Chancellor Herbert York.

The Committee on the Establishment of a Law School, chaired by Herbert York, spent nine months studying the matter, and reported in late 1982 that "A law school is an important scholarly and educational resource for UCSD and the community it serves" and that "Merger with California Western School of Law could result in a law school at UCSD appropriate to our scholarly and teaching misson."

The Ad Hoc Committee on the School of Law of the UCSD faculty Senate then reported to the Senate that the conclusions and recommendations of the York committee provided a firm basis for proceeding with negotiations to acquire California Western School of Law and urged the administration to begin the task as soon as possible.

Thereupon, the law school Board of Trustees made a formal written proposal of merger under the terms of which the law school would agree to transfer its considerable assets to the university on the condition that the Regents of the university would agree to maintain a law school of at least 500 students, of no less quality than required for membership in the Association of American Law Schools and accreditation by the American Bar Association, to be known as the California Western School of Law of the University of California at San Diego. The proposal contained appropriate conditions regarding the protection of the contract rights of the present Cal Western faculty and the expectation that distinguished professors qualified to teach law would supplement or replace current faculty, as well as a recitation of the advantages of such a merger to both institutions and to the community of southern California. In vain hope I drafted a suggested form of "Consortium" agreement!

Both the San Diego *Union* and the *Tribune* published editorials strongly urging the merger. However, despite a great deal of speculation, of questions of methodology, location and finance, with most people in both schools favoring the establishment of California Western as the law school of UCSD, the efforts were unsuccessful. It soon became painfully clear that the politics of the times would make the merger impossible.

Other University of California campuses also sought law schools, the two other San Diego law schools were vehemently opposed (as they had been to the almost forgotten effort by Hastings law school to purchase California Western), and the University of California Regents and legislature were clearly not in favor of any further use of tax monies to educate lawyers.

When it was recognized that the going would be extremely difficult if not impossible, the California Western Board of Trustees formally withdrew its offer of merger, and all thinking returned to the reality of the law school's future as an independent institution and the need to concentrate on solving its own problems and providing for its own needs.

With the return to that reality came my conviction that the best way for California Western to compete for top students with the older and more prestigious schools, and prepare them for good jobs out of school, was for California Western to specialize in one or two areas in which it could have the best programs, attract the best teachers—be the best. And trial practice seemed to me to be a natural because there was as yet a minimum of competition in that area from other law schools.

The faculty Curriculum Committee attacked the problem, and got as far as recommending seven areas of concentration or emphasis. The entire faculty, however, elected not to go in the direction of establishing one or two areas of specialization for the school. They chose instead, from among the recommendations of the Curriculum Committee, to approve five areas of concentration: commercial law, international law, advocacy and dispute resolution, tax law, and public law. Students were to take fourteen to seventeen class hours of instruction in their area of concentration. With that compromise, my notion of a true specialization at which the school would excel and for which it would be widely known was not to be.

But with compromise there resulted continued improvement of the law school. Along with the new areas of concentration the curriculum grew, the faculty wrote more, published more, and both led and participated in local and national activities enhancing their own and the school's reputation. Above all, however, Friesen and the faculty recognized that providing our students with the best possible instruction through good teaching was the greatest strength of our law school. The entire faculty emphasized improving their own teaching and helping each other to do so as well.

Just weeks before I left private practice I filed a lawsuit on behalf of a client named Shasteen, who had for years been in the cosmetics business. Recognizing that there was a market for a really good women's foot cream, Shass (as she was called) had found and purchased the formula of a Philadelphia woman who had developed an unusually effective vanishing foot cream. Shass contracted with a major manufacturer to compound the product to her specifications, and package and ship it to her customers. She had built a sales organization which sold the product nationwide.

In a short time, however, sales fell and customers began returning the product as unsatisfactory. Convinced that the manufacturer had somehow adulterated the product and so destroyed her business, Shass had asked me to proceed against them. Because the Statute of Limitations had almost run, suit had to be filed promptly. When I left the firm to teach at California Western, the case was assigned to Mark O'Neill, a handsome young partner who was a tough and effective litigator, often called the "baby-faced killer." Although he had almost exclusively defended personal injury suits on behalf of our insurance company clients, good lawyer that he was he gallantly agreed to handle this plaintiff's business case.

At least two years after I had left the office, Mark wrote me a letter about it. A propos of seeking the most effective ways to educate our students, I often read them Mark's letter. It was such a classic demonstration of how a good attorney and ethical practitioner had actually acted that I felt it was an unusual teaching tool. I hoped it would provide the students with an excellent example which they might emulate. A copy of that letter follows:

"This afternoon Miss Shasteen signed a release for $25,000, and I expect to receive the check next week. I was a little reluctant to advise you of the settlement until the money was actually in hand, the defendant's behavior has been that peculiar. However, it now looks as though we are going to be paid, and I therefore feel reasonably confident in reporting on the settlement as an almost-accomplished fact.

"This has been a strange case—one of the most unusual and certainly the most difficult and challenging I have ever worked on.

"As of last August Shass had been deposed in infinitesimal detail in a deposition that took a day and a half and covered 175 pages of transcript. I had deposed the custodian of Strong Cobb's records and had received an enormous quantity of documentary mish-mash, all of it in difficult to read xerox, and much of it in longhand entries. A typewritten memo was an unspeakable luxury that I would read and re-read in a spirit of sybaritic self indulgence. I organized in batches that which related to various production runs.

"I then received from Shass all of her correspondence with Strong Cobb, with Betty Curtis (Shass' employee), with customers, and I arranged this stuff chronologically. I then prepared an abstract of all this stuff, production run by production run, and I correlated Shass' deposition testimony *and* the invoices *and* Strong Cobb's answers to interrogatories with all this. By the time all this was done I had a general overview of the problem, enough to give me a feeling for the broad outlines of the case's settlement value, but still not a very firm handle on it from the standpoint of trial presentation.

"I knew by this time that there was some merit to Shass' contention. I also knew that it was hardly a black and white situation, and there were persistent suggestions that Shass somehow suspected, or maybe knew, and maybe ratified or acquiesced in the adulterating changes Strong Cobb was making in the product.

"One piece of evidence was particularly worrisome. I mentioned it to you and emphasized it, at your suggestion, to Shass—a letter she wrote to Strong Cobb just before the last batch was made. She abjured them to follow the formula to a T, but she added, 'using minimum amount of wax.' This letter meant only one thing: she had to have known that they were using wax, and she clearly acquiesced in their use of at least a 'minimum amount' of it.

"With this concern very much in mind I came to the conclusion that we would probably be doing Shass a great favor if we could settle this matter for $15,000 to $20,000, and I recall that you concurred. It was apparent to me, unfortunately, that Shass was thinking of this case as a vehicle for getting rich. While she was ultimately a most reasonable and gracious client, there was a rather long period in which she was demanding, irascible and romantic in her notions about the settlement potential.

"I did my best early last fall, along about September, to get Strong Cobb to make me some kind of offer. They never did. I therefore pushed the matter to pretrial, and a conference was held late in December. The position adopted by Strong Cobb at that point probably turned out to have cost them dearly in the long run. They were tough, totally inhospitable and almost arrogant. They offered us—believe it or not—$500.

"At that point I really didn't care how the case came out. I simply knew we had to try it. *I wrote it off as a loser in my own mind, never expecting to see a dime, but determined to spare no expense or effort to give this lady the best representation she could get from anybody in this city. If I were to lose I didn't want Shass to say it was due to a halfhearted effort.*[33]

"I then went back to the Strong Cobb records and spent night after night with them. *I couldn't possibly think of spending office time on them, there was just too much time involved.*[34] There was a period of about six weeks in which I was spending a couple of hours almost every night, except weekends, analyzing the Strong Cobb records with a microscope. These analyses proved to me beyond any doubt that Shass' suspicions were right—the buggers were adding wax, and they seemed to be doing it in a half-assed way. There was no particular pattern to it. The amounts just got larger and larger.

"And the astonishing thing is that the records confirmed her statement that there was an agreement, rather early in the game, that the experiments with wax were a failure and that wax wouldn't be included in the product anymore. After this agreement was reached the next two production runs were made without wax. But thereafter, for reasons that the records did not make clear, wax started getting back into the batches, and with each production run a greater amount of wax was used. Finally, when they got to the point where they were in the four ounce size, the wax was really a very significant element in the total mix.

"Three production runs were made using heavily waxed mixtures, and this was approximately coincidental with a decline in sales. The problem remained to tie in the declining sales with the severe adulteration of the product. To do this I had to hit the road.

"We went up to Detroit to depose people from J.L. Hudson. All of the sales girls who were touted as good potential witnesses turned

---

[33] Italics added
[34] Italics added

out to be either total flops or utterly unavailable. Of the five people I was supposed to depose, I managed to get the testimony of only one—but she was an all-star. She was a buyer, a person of extraordinary intelligence, beautifully articulate, obviously impartial and objective—and when she confirmed that there was an apparent change in the quality of the product and that the decline in sales that her store experienced was coincident with the adulteration, Strong Cobb's counsel was visibly impressed.

"I flew to Philadelphia to take the deposition of one of the independent manufacturer's representatives who handled the product in that region. He too was a jewel. He was a man of integrity, very considerable experience, and he confirmed beyond any reasonable doubt that a change did occur in the product, that it would not penetrate the way it did before, that it did not do the job it did originally, and that many complaints and returns occurred after this change (which was principally noted in the four ounce size). Both of these witnesses testified that there was still a place in the market for Dekal. There were other competing creams, but Dekal, in their opinion, was an unusually effective product, and if adequate advertising campaigns were mounted it could sell.

"I then began to depose every Strong Cobb executive the records referred to. I didn't realize it at the time, but these depositions seemed to have the effect of physically wearing down the Strong Cobb brass. Four or five of these depositions were taken, and I don't believe that any lasted less than four hours. They were all based largely on their own documents and they confirmed beyond any doubt their addition of wax to the product. Moreover, they very clearly suggested that this incorporation of wax was without Shass' knowledge or consent. It was apparent, finally, that the consciences of the Strong Cobb people were being pricked. I could see that this wax thing was a sore point. I was also developing the basis for an argument that their manufacturing methods were primitive, imprecise, inconsistent and inherently productive of variations in the end result.

"The case was scheduled for trial on Monday, June 21. On the Thursday before trial Thompson Hine offered me $10,000. Shass rejected it flatly and told me she would prefer to lose her share of it and get nothing than accept such an amount without a further struggle. My feeling was the same. On the morning of trial Strong Cobb came up to $20,000. At this point I was at $30,000, and the trial judge put very heavy pressure on both of us to get together. After a great deal of telephoning to California, where Strong Cobb's parent resides (International Chemical and Nuclear) an agreement was finally reached on $25,000 payable immediately.

(How much bigger those numbers were in 1971 than they sound today!)

"I would like you to know that one of the most incredible things about this whole story is that the petition you drafted, at a time when you were undoubtedly shooting in the dark, and your shots were based exclusively on what the client said, turned out to be a masterpiece, not one word of which I wished to change. So many times the petition comes home to haunt plaintiff's counsel, usually during closing argument. Yours was a beauty. It had the perfect blend of specificity and generality. The essential theory was still sound—they added wax without the plaintiff's permission or consent, and they failed to produce the product they agreed to make. The theories were also just as good as ever—negligence in the manufacturing process and breach of contract.

"All in all, I am pleased with the settlement. Shass is 65 years old, and I think it is much better to have a relatively small bird in the hand than a couple of turkeys in the bush. A judgment would certainly have been appealed, and it might well have been another couple of years before Shass would have seen any money. She very desperately needs money. She wants to get back into production. I think this will enable her to do so. Most important of all, she seems genuinely pleased and satisfied. She feels vindicated, and she likes the way they had to eat humble pie at the end.

"I must confess there were many days when I was sorry I ever heard of Shasteen Ltd. or Dekal. In the end, however, it turned out to be a great adventure. It was especially satisfying to represent a plaintiff for a change—a real, warm flesh and blood client instead of an insurer. I am grateful to you for the chance to have had this experience."

What more articulate real-life model could one find for law students than this letter describing the efforts of an ethical, conscientious and able lawyer on behalf of his client?

Through the good offices of Dennis Avery while he was associate dean under Ernie Friesen, California Western administered a most unusual program. Major cash awards were given by the Durfee Foundation, established by Avery's family, to individuals who have enhanced the dignity of others through legal institutions. Durfee Foundation award winners were such remarkable people as Ruth S. Murphy Casselman, founder and president of the American Immigration and Citizenship Conference, Eugenio Velasco, Chilean lawyer and civil rights activist during the regime of Salvadore Allende, Carlyle Hall, Jr., founder of the Center for Law in the Public Interest in Los Angeles, and Professor Anthony Amsterdam, advocate for the abolition of capital punishment.

The judges in 1983 included UCSD Chancellor Richard Atkinson, Joan Bernstein, former HEW general counsel, Robert Macfarlane, Jr., Durfee Foundation managing director, and law school faculty member Justice William Grimes.

Also in 1983 came my second sabbatical leave from the law school, now far more calm and secure than at the time of my first. The bleakness of my personal life with the tragic loss in 1969 of my only child, Diane, followed by Toni's death just ten years later had magically changed by my courtship and marriage to Martha Austin Cockrell, a lovely widow from Abilene, Texas. In late September Martha and I set off on a bold adventure to the Orient. The professional aspect of the trip was to be a study of the oriental methods of determining facts and truth in legal proceedings. Chin Kim, the law school Library Director, had helped arrange several remarkable introductions and interviews for me, recollections of which may properly be a part of the California Western story.

The first such interview was to be with a University of Beijing law professor. Armed with one piece of paper on which was written in Chinese the name and address of the State Guest House where we were staying and another with the name of the law professor at the University of Beijing, I confidently hailed a taxi. After I had shown the paper with the law school address, the woman driver drove interminably until we entered what appeared to be a university campus and finally stopped in front of a gray-looking building among many other gray-looking buildings. Until I was reasonably certain I'd find my man and not need her to take me back to the Guest House, I hesitated to pay her. When she indicated the amount of the fare I raised my hand to signal that she should wait.

Entering the building I could find no one, and all the office doors seemed to be locked. I came back outside to find the taxi-driver loudly complaining for her fare to several people who had gathered. In vain I tried, in broken French, German and Spanish, even in the few words I remembered of Japanese learned in language school during World War II, to make myself understood. In desperation, I said something in Hungarian—and unbelievably a man responded! He assured me they would be able to call another cab so I paid the woman, by then almost in tears, and she happily drove off.

My new friend entered the building and apparently was able to call or alert someone. Soon a man rode up on a bicycle and introduced himself to me in English as the professor with whom I had the appointment. We had a most interesting conversation which lasted more than two hours, covering many subjects, from his exposure to the determination of facts in the Chinese courts and what they taught in Chinese law schools to the unhappy plight of Communist law professors.

An interview had been arranged for me in Thailand, a difficult one with Judge Pompetch Wichitcholchai of the Ministry of Justice. For obvious reasons I promptly suggested we be on a first name basis—and luckily he spoke enough English for me to gain some valuable information from him in an informal and cordial visit.

Another interview was in Singapore, the legendary city/state with its exotic mixture of Chinese, Indians, Europeans, Eurasians, Pakistani and Malaysians. Al-Mansor Adabi was a remarkable man who was the Managing Director of the Malay Law Journal, a leading legal publisher in the Orient. He provided me with an insight into the universitality of my subject and the problems which confront oriental lawyers in determining and presenting factual truths in legal proceedings, and the efforts of law publishers to satisfy their needs.

Interviews with two appellate judges of the Osaka District Court in Japan had been arranged through Professor Zentaro Kitigawa of Kyoto University. Martha accompanied me on the interviews and luncheon in Osaka with Justices Masahiro Iseki and Shintaro Kato. They were unusually suave, friendly to us both, and spoke fluent English. In a long and pleasant meeting they provided interesting and informative views of Japanese court procedures. That evening the professor insisted that we join him and his family at a dinner being given for one of the school's leading donors. Why were we so reminded of home?

The rich donor turned out to be the highlight of the evening. A pompous little man, he spoke just enough English to brag about everything he had and had done. He even actually tried to put his hand on Martha's leg and suggested that we have dinner with him alone the following evening. On the back of his calling card was a tiny photograph of his grand home, and he gave everyone at the table several little gifts!

Following a delightful stay in Kyoto at tiny and quaint Chikiriya Inn, known as a *ryokan*, we left that most lovely and interesting city for Tokyo. There four interviews had been arranged, the first of which was to be the most memorable.

In the morning of the day we were to meet, I telephoned Hideo Masamoto, with whom I had been in correspondence. Masamoto was the Chief Liaison Officer of the General Secretariat of the Supreme

Court of Japan, a court of fourteen justices and a chief justice. It was he who had arranged for my meeting with Justice Masami Ito. Just as we were about to set the time for the interview, I took a courageous step.

"Mrs. Gafford is with me here at the Imperial Hotel, and I wonder whether it would be all right for her to accompany me in my meeting with Justice Ito?"

There followed what could only be described as a pregnant pause. What a spot he must have been in. But he rose to the occasion.

"I am sure Justice Ito would be happy to have Mrs. Gafford accompany you."

As we entered the great white marble building we were completely alone. There was not a soul to be seen as we signed the guest book on a stand at the bottom of the grand stairway. The last American name we found in it was United States Supreme Court Justice Tom C. Clark! Upon ascending the broad white stairway with its stark tan marble walls we were greeted by Mr. Masamoto. He was a good-looking gentleman with eyeglasses and graying hair, dressed in a dark blue suit, with a white shirt and a conservative tie. He could have been a partner in an American law firm.

As Mr. Masamoto led us into Justice Ito's suite, we saw three secretaries sitting before typewriters at their desks. They looked at us (especially Martha) as if we were aliens from another planet. It was apparent to me that they'd never before seen a woman ushered into the Justice's chambers. I will never know how or what Chin Kim did to have been able to arrange this for me.

Justice Ito greeted us warmly. A slight man with even features and a ready smile, he too was dressed in western clothing and motioned for us to be seated in a grouping of a sofa and three easy chairs around a low table at one end of the room. Beautifully carpeted, the room was enormous, perhaps thirty or forty feet long, and at its other end was the Justice's desk with two straight chairs in front of it.

We were introduced to a nice-looking young man, one of the Justice's law clerks who spoke English. Judging from the way Mr.

Masamoto was treated it was obvious that he was a high-ranking official, far superior in rank to the law clerks. He remained in the room
with us during the interview and apparently had arranged for someone to bring in tea and rice cakes shortly after we sat down.

The interview was fascinating. The Justice was completely forth-
coming in all his answers, seemed to know far more about American
law than I did about Japanese, and was absolutely charming. Near
the end of the interview, Martha spoke up.

"Justice Ito, are there any women judges in Japan?"

The Justice seemed to ponder the question after it was translated
for him. He turned to his clerk who had been acting as our interpreter
and spoke for some time in Japanese. The law clerk responded and
Masamoto joined in the discussion. Ultimately the Justice turned to
Martha and the law clerk translated his words.

"Yes, there are two."

"In all of Japan?"

"Yes, but they are chief judges."

After a bit more discussion it was revealed that on two three-judge
panels of a lower court the women were the seniors!

When it came time to leave, the Justice asked through the interpreter where we were going next and whether he could be of any assistance to us.

"You are most gracious, sir. We now have an appointment with
Dean Hideo Tanaka of the University of Tokyo law school. Would it
be possible for a taxi to be called for us?"

"Oh, no. You would honor me if you will allow me to have my
driver take you there."

Thereupon we were shown to a doorway at the back of the building by Mr. Masamoto. A black sedan drew up under the *porte cochere*
and a uniformed chauffeur opened its door for us. There were fresh
flowers in small cut-glass vases on either side of the back seat, and
lace doilies on the headrests.

The interview with Dean Tanaka was not nearly as pleasant as
with Justice Ito. The Dean was abrupt of speech and severe in appear-

ance—actually we both thought he looked just like the cruel Japanese army officers portrayed in American World War II movies!

There was an interpreter who spoke rather halting English and it seemed to us that Dean Tanaka wanted to answer all questions in as few words as possible. Nevertheless I did gain some valuable perspective on Japanese law schools and the way law was taught. But most interesting was a question put by Martha:

"Dean, how many women students are there in your law school?"

The answer was short and direct.

"None. Law school too difficult for women. They could not pass Bar."

End of discussion. End of interview.

In July of 1984, the continuing faculty concerns and dissatisfaction with the administration of the law school resulted in the appointment of a committee to study the school's administrative structure. By September there were meetings to discuss methods for electing new trustees and to consider possible nominees.

With the acceptance of the fact that the UCSD merger was unlikely and that law school applications nationwide were falling, came deep concerns for the school's financial health. Both the Board and the faculty were looking more closely at the school's financial statements. One study asserted that over the previous five years the school had received an average of $17,000 a year in total contributions of alumni and others. At the same time, conservative estimates of annual expenditures of the office primarily charged with the responsibility of obtaining contributions, exclusive of any provision for pension, during those five years were $180,000 a year, increased to $240,000 during the then current year.

It was asserted that in the light of ever-reducing student population and consequently reduced tuition income, the school could not bear dual administrative costs. In the autumn of 1984, under the able leadership of Judge Frank Orfield as Chairman of the Board of Trustees, further steps in the "transition" of the administration of the law school were effected. By mutual consent, President Castetter announced his intention to retire effective in the fall of 1985, but with the responsibility for all financial affairs of the school to be transferred to Dean Friesen immediately.

In the fall of 1985, a committee headed by Professor Marilyn Ireland made objections and recommendations respecting new suggested by-laws drafted by the Board of Trustees. These excerpts from that report, attached to the minutes of a faculty meeting, reflect the faculty mood:

"The by-law changes proposed at the August 28 Board meeting do not abolish the office of President. Rather they change the name of that office to Dean...California Western School of Law is an academic institution, not a sole business proprietorship.

"...The faculty had hoped, with the resignation of President Castetter, that the perception of this institution as 'one man's show' might expire...Instead, the proposal to place the 'Dean' on the Board threatens a return to the situation that existed here some years ago, when the Board's only source of information was a 'Dean/President' whom it was legally and morally obligated to oversee. In such a milieu, facts rapidly degenerate into generalized personal reassurances that 'all is well', and personal friendship replaces sound judgment. Because of the size of the law school, it is advisable to combine the functions of academic leadership and managerial leadership in one office. That such an officer should also be accountable to him or herself as trustee raises a substantial question of propriety.

"The merger of the Chief Financial Officer with the Deanship contains a similar pitfall. Management, to be effective, should be financially accountable, as a matter of routine, to someone other than itself...In fact, the office has always been vacant or filled with an officer whose employment was at the sole discretion of management. The result was a total breakdown of fiscal control...The faculty does not want a weak Dean. It wants a strong Dean who shares with it a commitment to a sound academic program. Accountability does not produce weakness, it produces strength. The Dean ought not to be accountable to himself as trustee, nor as Chief Financial Officer. The Dean ought to be accountable as a sound manager to an independent board. The Dean ought not to be accountable only to himself as to the maintaining of financial records that identify management expenditures."

The faculty's concerns were properly addressed.

In his six years as dean, after which he had indicated his wish to return to teaching, Friesen had fulfilled most admirably his role as liaison between what had in the perception of the faculty and others been too much a "one man's show" to a substantial and well-managed independent institution. Recognizing the need for a more structured administration, he had appointed Robert Cane as Associate Dean for Administration. Cane in turn brought in Nancy Ramsayer to set up for the first time a truly efficient Admissions Office. Mary Jo Riley had brought in Linda North (later Dews), who forged a well-managed Placement operation.

The school had now reached another threshold from which new impetus in major fund-raising, improved relations with the American Bar Association, strong student recruitment, better organization and prudent fiscal management were needed to raise the school to the next plateau.

The first key had to be the election to the Board of several new members who would supply a variety of knowledge and expertise, responsible independence, and sources of financial resources which would provide not only the contributions but also the example so necessary for successful fund-raising. We began by approaching some of our friends and were fortunate soon to recruit several people of substance who were civic leaders and involved with other educational and cultural institutions in the community.

After a brief stint as Chairman, Fred Schrupp had to resign for health reasons. Judge Zenoff became Chairman of the Board. Under his wise counsel both the complexion of the board and the school were much changed. At my urging, some of my close friends, active and influential people, were added. Reverend Lawrence Waddy had taught at UCSD, written extensively and long been associated with Saint James by the Sea Episcopal Church and numerous charitable causes. Veryl Fredericksen was an active and successful business-woman and civic leader, Hal Stephens was another important civic leader who headed Mission Federal Credit Union, and Dr. Robert Epsten was a noted physician and community leader.

Dr. Robert Doede had been a successful entrepreneur, was an important money manager and member of numerous boards, while James Lorenz headed a major law firm and Craig McClellan was a prominent trial lawyer. Former faculty member Murray Galinson had become the successful president of the San Diego National Bank and an active community leader, and Ballard Smith, head of a large catering company, was former president of the San Diego Padres.

Of the earlier board members, Sam Thurman, former Dean of the University of Utah Law School remained active, along with Jim West, a prominent CPA and one of the city's leaders, who serves loyally to this day. Board members Darrell Holmes, former president of Northern Colorado University, Albert Johnson, Vice President of San Diego State University, and George Andreos, alumni president, served their last year.

Invited to serve on the Board after my retirement from the faculty in 1986, I was able to observe and participate in the development and many changes in the law school under a self-reliant Board infused with the new strength, resources and enthusiasm of such outstanding people. The pattern had now been established for a strong, active and independent Board, having an excellent relationship with the faculty as well as mutual respect. It was the perfect setting for a new Dean—and new hope!

Chapter XIII

A Different Kind of Dean and a New Era

Nineteen eighty-six was the year that the space shuttle "Challenger" exploded on take-off, killing all seven crew members. It was the year of the world's worst nuclear accident at Chernobyl in the U.S.S.R. and of Ferdinand Marcos' flight from the Philippines. National Security Adviser John Poindexter and Col. Oliver North pleaded the Fifth Amendment in the "Irangate" scandal, Prince Andrew and Sarah Ferguson were married, becoming the Duke and Duchess of York, and the oil surplus forced its price down to $10 a barrel. The Musee d'Orsay opened in the old Gare d'Orsay railroad station in Paris, and death came to Cary Grant, Rudy Vallee, Wallis Warfield Simpson (the Duchess of Windsor), as well as the great English sculptor, Henry Moore.

The faculty search for a new dean followed the orthodox lines of accepting resumes from professors, deans and administrators of other law schools, many of whom were extremely attractive and likely candidates. Only one unusual candidate appeared however, a man who had taught law part time and done some legal writing, but whose career had been primarily as a practicing attorney and in-house counsel with strong business experience and connections. To many of the faculty such a background was suspect, certainly for a faculty member and perhaps even more so for a dean.

While he was not the first choice of the search committee, to those on the Board who knew him and to a very few of us on the faculty, his availability at that moment seemed serendipitous. It was very clear that the school was academically sound, and that what was needed was a strong, experienced hand at business and public relations, but with sufficient academic credentials to be able to work with a law school faculty.

Michael H. Dessent was a graduate of Northwestern University where he earned his B.A. and J.D. degrees, and was a member of the Order of Coif. He had been an associate with Gray, Cary, Ames and Frye, then San Diego's largest law firm, after which he was General Counsel for Central Federal Savings and Loan, next Fotomat Corporation and for the last several years for the Price Club, an exceptionally successful multi-billion dollar San Diego-based business. He was a strong supporter of such major cultural organizations as the Old Globe, San Diego Museum of Art and Mingei Folk Art Museum, was an avid baseball fan, and had a wide circle of friends and acquaintances in San Diego.

Although his appointment as dean was ultimately recommended to the Board by the faculty, it was not without considerable difficulty and strong urging by me as a retiring faculty member both personally and by letter. Upon the faculty's recommendation, the Board of Trustees readily approved, and a proper contract was negotiated between Dessent and Judge Zenoff as Chairman of the Board.

From the beginning, it was evident that Dessent was exactly what California Western needed at that time. One of his first acts, completely novel and unorthodox, was to have a video tape of the school professionally prepared. The tape showed the school facilities, members of the faculty and student body, and many of the physical and cultural attractions of San Diego and environs—all very well and tastefully done. For surprisingly little money, hundreds of copies of the tape were made and sent to career advisors of colleges all over the country, as well as to geographically-selected law school alumni who were persuaded to show the video to prospective students in their areas. Over 3000 prospective students saw it in the first year!

In addition to the video, Dessent took another unorthodox action: he traveled on the student recruitment road himself. As he remarked to me, "It was really extraordinary. At those student recruitment meetings, the kids were actually wide-eyed at our school's table when they found out I was the dean. All the other schools had admissions people or faculty members—it really seemed to make an impression."

In four months of 1986 Dessent traveled 50,000 miles on student recruitment, and several members of the faculty traveled many thousands more.

The results were astounding. Applications for admission in the following years increased dramatically, allowing for both increase in enrollment and the luxury of selecting students with appreciably higher credentials than before. At the same time, Dessent was somehow able to achieve remarkably good publicity for the school and himself in the media of San Diego and elsewhere, soon increasing both the name recognition and reputation of a school whose excellence previously seemed to have been a well-kept secret.

There were also some great additions to the faculty such as Michal Belknap, a distinguished historian turned lawyer, Howard Berman, noted human rights advocate, and Lawrence Benner, nationally recognized authority on indigent criminal defense services. With increased income, the school was able to raise faculty compensation, making it possible both to retain its best faculty members and attract desirable new ones.

Succeeding me in teaching advocacy skills was Janeen Kerper, a nationally known authority in her field. Under Professors Kerper, Lynch, Ehrlich, Noyes, Smith, Motley, Cox, Stiglitz and other faculty members who assisted, California Western's trial teams continued the tradition of excellence. Our winning record was surpassed by the success of six regional victories and ultimately a national title in trial practice.

On Cal Western's first trip to the National Administrative Law Moot Court competition, its team coached by Professor Smith and others won second place in the national finals, judged by a panel presided over by Supreme Court Justice Antonin Scalia. Under the coaching of Professor Lynch, California Western won the national championship in the National Moot Court competition, the prestigious granddaddy of law school competitions.

There was a new energy and electricity in the school which was contagious. With the appointment of Judy Kachaylo as Alumni Director, there were stronger and stronger ties to the alumni and greatly increased giving. Many thousands of dollars were raised at an Alumni Association Casino Night. Martha and I donated as the main raffle prize the classic Fiat convertible which had once been my daughter Diane's. How happy it would have made her.

Among the management tools learned from business, the new dean instituted an incentive program for the faculty which raised some eyebrows but proved very effective. Monetary rewards were given for law review articles published, books written and academic conferences conducted. In one year alone the school held widely-publicized and well-attended conferences involving renowned experts on Sports Law, Biotechnology, Entertainment Law, and Law and the Arts.

Many new and important friends of the law school were made by the appointment of a Council of Visitors, and in 1987 the school received its first major grant of $400,000 to establish the Al Simon Center for Telecommunications Law. One of the initial telecommunications law programs in the nation was created at Cal Western by the Center under the direction of Professor Carl Hilliard.

The first major improvement of the law school facility under Dean Dessent was the conversion of the former auditorium on the third floor of the school into a magnificent large new classroom, and considerable monies were raised by the sale of name plaques on the seats. New Cal Western wear was introduced in the bookstore, as well as all manner of utility, sports and gift items, even license plate holders, with the school name or logo—all creating a greater awareness and camaraderie among students, faculty and staff.

In the *Alumni Quarterly* for the spring and summer of 1988 it was reported that the Advocacy Honors Board had sent eleven different competition teams on the road and hosted the first National Telecommunications Law Moot Court competition. It also reported that two

Sophisters had coordinated the Gafford Trial Competition. It had been after testing several names and ideas that I had named the Advocacy Honors Board in the early seventies and named the students seeking to become members of the Board Sophisters. Seeing those creations prevail and blossom over the years has been a tremendous satisfaction—but the faculty having named the trial competition as they did after I retired was somewhat disconcerting.

An *Alumni Quarterly* also reported such items as the Judges' Night held at the law school, when the fifty-eight alumni who were on the Bench were honored, the appointment of Paul Gudel and Janet Bowermaster to the faculty, and that the 1988 fall class represented 37 states, the District of Columbia, Korea and Lebanon. Their academic credentials were the highest of any in recent years, 37% were women, and among their previous occupations were physicians, teachers, accountants, a landscape architect, a Navy SEAL, a retired college professor, a decorated Marine pilot, an Arabian horsebreeder, a psychiatrist, paralegals, a private detective, journalists, and a figure skater!

In late 1988 it was time to consider whether Dessent's three-year contract should be renewed. Since by then I had succeeded Judge Zenoff as Chairman of the Board of Trustees, it fell to me to learn the feelings of the faculty and the board and to negotiate with him. The response of the faculty was in a five-page letter to me signed by Katharine Rosenberry as Chair of the Faculty Executive Committee. It began by saying "The faculty unanimously recommends that Michael Dessent be reappointed as Dean with compensation to be determined by the Board and him, that he be given tenure as a professor of law (they had not approved professorial tenure when he was first appointed), and that he be given a sabbatical at the end of six years."

The letter further indicated that the untenured faculty had unanimously agreed with the recommendation of the tenured faculty, and "I am confident that we are the only law school in the country where every single faculty member strongly supports the Dean." There followed a remarkable recitation of accomplishments. "In a three year period Dean Dessent has led us from a significant deficit to a substantial surplus...he has created an endowment and development program...along with the Board's help, raised enough money to build a much needed classroom, created an awareness among the alumni that they should contribute money...Three years ago none of the faculty would have guessed that we would be strong enough financially to be seriously discussing constructing a building on the parking lot.

"...I think we had more newspaper articles mentioning California Western in his first year in office than we did in all the other years I was at the school...He has encouraged us to raise the visibility of the school...He has succeeded in getting more faculty members involved by taking an interest in what we are doing and supporting us...Even on small issues he responds...Another way in which he maintains such an excellent rapport with the faculty is by not playing favorites...Once again Dean Dessent has taken charge and is implementing a redecorating plan...Applications are up substantially and credentials are up (in major part because of his personal recruitment of students)...We appreciate the strong support given him by the Board. But it is his leadership that has made the accomplishments possible..."

Mike and I negotiated a new five-year contract at substantially increased compensation, clearly well-deserved. It contained alternative times for a sabbatical leave, depending upon the date of the anticipated regular ABA on-site inspection.

With his favorable extended contract, Dessent seemed to attack his mission with yet greater zeal and vigor. Even as the school's financial picture improved, we hired an expensive and experienced Development Director, and new fund-raising campaigns were instituted.

During the years of my tenure as Chairman several strong new members were added to the Board of Trustees who made substantial contributions to the school's welfare. Roy Black had been head of the overseas division of Electronic Rentals Group, Ltd., a billion-dollar Irish corporation, and then came to California to found Video Library, of which he was chairman. Connie Clapp was an alumna who had been Vice President in the Municipal Finance Department of

Goldman Sachs and Co., and Roy Bell was an alumnus who had become the successful head of a major San Diego law firm.

Mary Walshok was Associate Vice Chancellor of UCSD, Barry McComic was Chairman of RBMcComic, Inc. developers, after having been CEO of Avco Community Development, and Judith Haller was another successful alumna, a Superior Court Judge who became a Justice of the California Court of Appeal. Alfred Goodwin was Chief Judge of the United States Court of Appeals, and James Cobble was Dean of the Graduate Division of San Diego State University. Mark Mandell was another alumnus and practicing attorney, adjunct law professor, lecturer on real property finance and successful real estate developer.

As each department of the school was being strengthened, the business office was placed under experienced leadership when Lenore Frega joined the staff as Chief Financial Officer. She had earned her CPA in New Jersey, had been employed at Deloitte, Haskins and Sells, and had formerly been controller of a large construction company. At about the same time, Trustee Roy Black accepted the chairmanship of the Development Committee, and Jonnie Estell joined the law school staff and began her remarkably successful career in the newly-created post of Director of Minority Affairs.

Advancing further, the law school was able to attract two brilliant new minority professors, Christine Hickman and Andrea Johnson, both graduates of Harvard Law School. And Dean Dessent was able to report in the 1990-1991 *California Western News* that in the past four years Cal Western applicants had increased from 1200 to 3000, California bar passage rate had risen from 15th to 8th in the state, an $800,000 refurbishing/remodeling of the law school's historical building had been completed, the Annual Fund increased from $7,000 to $250,000, student-faculty ratio had been improved by hiring 22 new professors for a total of 37, all of the school's debt had been paid off and a major cash endowment program had been founded.

With everything at the school upbeat and favorable, an incredible diversion of even greater promise occurred. It all began when

Dessent happened to encounter a man and a young woman wandering into the main lobby of the school.

"Can I help you? I'm Dean Dessent."

"Oh, thank you very much. May I introduce myself. My name is Ameer Khan, and this is my daughter who is planning to go to law school."

Thereupon Dessent spent about half an hour conducting the two through the law school and singing its praises as only he could do, after which they departed. Some months passed and the dean received a check for $8000 drawn to the order of the law school by Ameer Khan. Naturally assuming that the check had been sent by a happy father upon his daughter's admittance to Cal Western, he sent an appropriate letter of appreciation. When another check in a somewhat smaller amount was received a few months later, Dessent checked the student files to see how the girl was doing, only to find there was no Khan on the student roster.

He called to tell me the strange story. "This is most extraordinary. I of course am going to write another thank you to him, but perhaps as chairman you might want to write Mr. Khan too and maybe find out what he's about."

Following some correspondence between us, Ameer Khan came again to San Diego. He told us that his daughter had decided to go to another law school in Texas where they lived, but that he had been so impressed with California Western and with its dean that he wanted to do what he could to help the school. He spoke expansively of his financial success as the owner-operator of retirement facilities in Houston and in Canada and of his close friendship with Sheikh Faiz Al-Abideen. He told us that Sheikh Faiz was a very close friend of the Crown Prince of Saudi Arabia and an important advisor to the King.

Before long additional three and four figure contributions were made to the school by Ameer, until one day he called to tell me that the Sheikh was in the United States on business and he would like to bring him to San Diego. There was the strong suggestion that some arrangement could be made with the Sheikh for Saudi Arabian financing of a new law school library in the millions of dollars if some teaching of Islamic law could be introduced into the curriculum.

On the night of Faiz' arrival, Martha and I were to attend a black tie affair at La Valencia Hotel in La Jolla. The party was sponsored by the Colleagues (an organization of which Martha was a member), which supported the Stuart Collection of sculptures on the UCSD campus. When Faiz learned of our plans, he immediately indicated his desire to attend. Ameer rushed him to his room at the Westgate Hotel, Faiz donned formal attire, and they met us at the party.

The guests seemed delighted with the Sheikh, who was a bespectacled young man with a dark beard, in black suit and gleaming white shirt under a red and white checked burnoose held on his head by a black velvet crown. Luba Johnston happily posed on his arm for photographers, and the newspapers dutifully reported our attendance "with a titled guest from Saudi Arabia, Sheikh Faiz Al-Abideen!"

While almost everything Faiz said was very vague, he spoke constantly of his belief that the Saudis would be interested in a substantial presence in our law school, made several allusions to sums of money in the millions for a building, and was consistently charming and optimistic. After meetings with Mike O'Keefe and Katharine Rosenberry of the faculty, and with Mike Dessent and me, Ameer and Faiz suggested that I reduce our mutual thoughts to writing. Because of their vagueness, those "thoughts" were difficult to express.

It had slowly become evident that Faiz and Ameer were to receive a finder's fee or commission on any Saudi moneys raised by them. The "Memorandum of Understanding" I drafted was among the "Law School", Faiz as the "Organizer", and Ameer as the "Facilitator". It spoke of the future activities of the Organizer and Facilitator in providing contributions of money and services for the Law School from Saudi Arabia and other Middle Eastern countries, and of the Law School's furtherance of American understanding of Middle Eastern culture and Islamic law, and promoting the exchange of students, faculty and ideas.

Organizer was promptly to provide to the Law School his curriculum vitae containing the usual and appropriate biographical information, names, positions and addresses of references. Upon the provision and acceptance of that information, the Facilitator and Organizer were to begin their efforts to obtain contributions to the law school for a period of six months, at which time the relationships of the parties were to be reviewed.

It was recited that it was the desire of the parties that the sum of $20,000,000 be raised for the Law School, although it was recognized that it would be unlikely that that sum would be raised within six months.

It was agreed however that the Law School would reward the Organizer and Facilitator together by paying them thirty percent of whatever amounts were received in cash by the Law School as a result of their efforts during the next six months. As and when $10,000,000 cash was received, steps would promptly be taken to appoint an appropriate faculty member and establish an institute offering Islamic law.

As further contributions were received and favorable Middle Eastern relationships established, appropriate steps would be taken leading to the exchange of students and faculty and the election of Organizer and outstanding Muslims and prominent figures of other cultures to the Council of Visitors and to provide other honorary recognition to deserving members of the international community. The memorandum was made subject to the approval of the entire Board of Trustees. Nobody ever signed the memorandum, and the Board never saw it.

The propriety and morality of paying 30% commission for the obtaining of contributions shocked and worried us. Such a figure sounded on the high side of the usual costs of raising money for institutions such as ours. Yet rightly or wrongly, the source of the money—Saudi oil millions—seemed somehow to allay any moral concern. We wondered whether there really was a moral issue, especially when both Ameer and Faizal told us of the extravagances and pomp and circumstance of the Saudi court.

While thoughts of Saudi millions enriching the Law School were dancing in our heads, no appointments (both Faizal and Ameer had very much wanted to become members of the Board of Trustees) or announcements were made. Although Ameer had actually made gifts of many thousands of dollars and preliminary checking had disclosed him to be what he said he was—and he did vouch for Faizal, for whom we had done nothing—we all felt somehow queezy. (Hence my requirement of Faizal's biographical data, which by the way was never received!)

Then about that time I received a telephone call from a man purporting to be Ameer's Canadian accountant who said that Ameer had directed him to send to Cal Western one-half the proceeds from the sale of his retirement home in Canada, proceeds which for tax reasons he would not otherwise be able to enjoy. The man's identity proved to be valid, there followed all sorts of telephone calls and inquiries regarding wire transfers and the like, wild speculations as to amounts up to several hundred thousand dollars, then a strange silence.

Finally, with considerable fanfare, it was arranged that Ameer and Faizal would come to San Diego when major announcements and presentations were to be made. With some anticipation, but at the same time with more than a little skepticism (how badly I wanted to believe) the day came. They both were here. Faizal, dark and handsome, acting profound and deliberate, was dressed in all his glory and made a colorful speech at the celebratory dinner.

He spoke in glowing terms of Dean Dessent and of me, of the glories of the school and its bright future and of its need for major contributions, of the glories of Islam, and of the need for mutual understanding and knowledge of the Islamic and American laws and cultures. He then urged that a great campaign be launched to accomplish these highest of aims, and announced that he was giving $1000 to touch it off. And he presented me with a copy of the Quran for the library!

Speechless and nonplussed, with great difficulty we thanked them both, and the following day they left. We never heard from Faizal again, although I did speak once or twice to Ameer who complained bitterly to me.

"You know, George, the man misled and hurt me far more than he misled you, and I don't know why. I enjoyed his hospitality in Riyadh and saw his closeness to the royal family. And you know, I sincerely believed that he was interested in helping the law school and would be able to do so with royal money. I knew he was selfish and saw this as a way to make a lot of money for himself. He was to get almost all of the 30%, but I didn't mind that as long as it would help Cal Western.

"You don't know it, but I even gave Faizal the little money he gave to the school and I have spent many thousand of dollars on him and on his travels. I paid his way here twice, once all the way from Saudi Arabia, out of my own pocket—all for naught! I am very sorry."

Neither Ameer's nor Faizal's motivations ever made any sense to us. Ameer's contributions were certainly appreciated, and there are I believe two chairs in the third floor new law school classroom with plaques indicating contributions by Faizal and Ameer. Except for our exchange of a Christmas card or two with Ameer after we last talked, I've heard nothing more from him. No doubt—wanting the dream—I had been the most gullible of all.

The mystery remains. Neither man ever received anything from us except maybe a meal or two, some drinks, and perhaps the doubtful honor of having meetings with a law school dean, two faculty members and the chairman of a board of trustees. Ameer did make the cash contributions—but beyond that the entire adventure and our pipe dream of Saudi millions for the law school had disappeared without explanation.

With or without Saudi aid, at the urging of Trustee Mark Mandell and somewhat guided by his expertise, more and more time and attention were given to the possibility of the law school's financing and erecting a building on the law school parking lot. Consideration and study were given to several kinds of development of the property for exclusive law school use, for partial law school use, or purely for investment.

The first proposal was for a low cost residential hotel, and among others were a law professional office building, a law school library, a high-rise office building, a law school faculty office and administration building, even a circular parking structure. Careful studies were made of the desirability and feasibility of each possibility. Ultimately, after weighing each proposal, after varied faculty and trustee opinions and many mind changes, the Board reached a decision.

It was to be a four-storey 34,000-square-foot Campus Center to house all deans, faculty and administrative offices, conference rooms, the bookstore and a deli. Along with further improvements to the main law school classroom and library building, this was determined to offer the most affordable and feasible means of fulfilling the most urgent needs of the law school as well as providing the best addition for the long term.

In July, 1992, ground was broken for the new 4.5 million-dollar building for the law school which seventeen years before could not pay its faculty salaries or the publishers of its library advance sheets and periodicals, and whose year-end operating results only six years before showed a deficit of over $660,000!

The experience and expertise of Trustee Connie Clapp, as well as her willingness to come repeatedly from New York and give so much of her time, were invaluable. Because of her, and the financial soundness of the school, it was possible to raise the $4.5 million through the sale of California tax-free bonds at a most favorable interest rate of less than 7%.

The expensive and highly-touted new development director, having failed to live up to expectations, was replaced by the lovely Mary Williams, her assistant. In well-managed and smooth-running campaigns, chaired by Roy Black and by Connie Clapp and Roy Bell, more than two million dollars were raised from trustees, faculty and alumni in a remarkable showing of loyalty and interest.

The school seemed to be truly on its way to the achievement of its recognition as one of the country's truly fine law schools. Success, as the saying goes, breeds success. Even before the new building was built the school was the recipient of its second major grant, accomplished through the efforts of Professor Lawrence Benner. Before San Diego County had established its Public Defender program, indigent accused had for some years been defended by a privately funded organization headed by one Alex Landon. His group through careful husbanding of its assets had accumulated a rainy-day fund of some $640,000. When its work was taken over by the county, it proposed using those funds to endow a deserving law school program. Professor Benner prepared a successful grant request on behalf of Cal Western proposing the creation of an Institute for Criminal Defense Advocacy to improve the administration of criminal justice, the protection of Constitutional rights and the delivery of defense services to indigent accused.

Professors Benner and Janeen Kerper were co-founders of the Institute, with Professor Kerper as its first Executive Director. Benner's concept has resulted in a unique national program which among other things conducts an annual training program known as the National Trial Skills Academy for lawyers providing defense to the indigent accused. The faculty, made up of the leading criminal defense attorneys in the nation, are all volunteers, with only their transportation and lodging paid for by the Institute. Cal Western students also benefit and learn from the program by doing the videotaping of the one-on-one training exercises, meeting with the faculty and attorney-students and helping with the logistics.

There was a renewed pride in the school by both faculty and students. Alumni reunions became regular and well-attended functions, Dessent's peripatetic pace went on unabated, contributions continued to grow, and improvements were constantly being made to the main building, known as 350 Cedar Street.

Fortunately too there had been a succession of efficient and well-liked associate deans, who much like the executive officers on

Navy ships often had unpopular duties, such as in the case of associate deans the giving of less than desirable tasks or course assignments to faculty and the disciplining of students. After Professors Leahy and O'Keefe during the earlier years had come Penn Lerblance and John Noyes, then more recently Jan Stiglitz and Katharine Rosenberry, followed by Bill Lynch, Scott Ehrlich, Phil Manns and Barbara Cox.

The Autumn 1991-1992 Alumni Quarterly had reported that the October Phonathon (which had become an annual event) raised $72,000, that there were now 14 applications for each first-year seat in the law school, that half the class were women, and that there were now 26% minority students in the school. Also reported was the retirement of Barbara Costley, the Registrar of the law school, and probably the one person best known and liked by more students than any other member of the faculty or administration. Costley had served the law school loyally, cheerfully and efficiently for thirty years. She somehow had managed to know personally just about every student who ever attended the school, and certainly they all knew her.

The school was operating with an annual budget of $14 million, and there were 4200 alumni in 50 states and 13 foreign countries. The San Diego Biotechnology Forum founded by California Western continued with its annual Biotechnology Conferences, and the first chapter of Lambda Alpha International Student Association was established at Cal Western with the help of Professor Richard Fink and Associate Dean Rosenberry, a member of Lambda Alpha International, an honorary association of land development professionals. The school's unusual Clinical Internship program's national reputation was growing, and regular conferences for U.S. and Mexican Federal judges were hosted by the International Legal Studies department.

The first class in the Master of Comparative Law program with Professor Chin Kim as its Director had awarded degrees to students from Korea, France, Saudi Arabia, Thailand and Kuwait in 1985. In the next seven years students attended the program from Sweden, Iceland, Switzerland, the Netherlands, Japan, China, Taiwan, Argentina, and Brazil.

The school's competition teams continued to excel in the Roger J. Traynor Moot Court Competition, the Jessup International Moot Court Competition, and the National Trial Competition. Professor Janet Bowermaster testified in congressional hearings and Professor Bohrer was named Visiting Scholar at UCSD. Professors Benner and Belknap, Stiglitz and Cox, Noyes, O'Keefe, Linda Morton and Glenn Smith, as well as Lerblance and Hilliard gained local and national recognition with speeches, publications, AALS section chairs, ABA inspection teams, editorial boards and conferences. Such participation and wide-spread activities well reflected the electricity and enthusiasm now pervading the school.

But much yet remained to be done.

*Justice Dave Zenoff and Dean
Ernie Friesen*

*Artist Doug Jones works on
unfinished portrait*

*Dean Mike Dessent and trustees attending
Commencement awarding honorary degree
to Justice Zenoff*

*From the Elks to the Masons, the Department of Motor Vehicles to USIU's School for
Performing Arts now California Western School of Law*

From the grandeur of the old ...

To the efficiency and color of the new administration and faculty office building

Dean Smith and Library Director Phyllis Marion cut the ribbon with the help of Security Guard James Rhodes and Trustees Ken Greenman and Jeff Lewin.

Entrance to library soon after the move from Point Loma

But this is the entrance to the new library building!

With its impressive exterior

Both hard cover and electronic research

With the still stately interior of the 350 Cedar Street building, now a Historical Landmark

Martha had been skeptical

Chapter XIV

Even a Dean's Honeymoon Ends

It cannot be doubted that during Mike Dessent's tenure as dean California Western School of Law truly came of age. Indeed, as later reported in a school publication, he "presided over the most productive decade in the school's history."

Certainly along with the many other accomplishments of the period, the new four-storey Campus Center provided the most significant physical improvement. In the words of its architect, the new Center's Roman arches, red tile roof, and balconies referenced "the existing building's late 1920's Neo-Renaissance style."

The Campus Center had a split-level piazza and its own signature campanile. A series of terraces led to both the first and second floors of the building as well as to the bookstore and deli, creating an outdoor campus retreat. In a most appropriate major fund-raising effort, an outpouring of affection for the Dean Emeritus by friends and alumni resulted in the naming of the Castetter Courtyard at the Center's entrance. Inside the building the administration and faculty offices were provided with large skylights and the most up-to-date fiber optics, multiple communications and data hook-ups. Parking was provided in an underground garage.

Any accreditation problems the school had had in years gone by were completely overcome and forgotten with the inspection by the American Bar Association which takes place every seven years. Mike O'Keefe, once again an excellent Associate Dean, had organized a 250-plus-page Faculty Self Study, which along with the scrutiny by the seven-member inspection team resulted in a reinforcement of the school's good standing with the ABA and the AALS.

In the law school library there were established in their honor the John M. DeBarr Military Law Collection, the Dwight E. Stanford Reading Room, the James E. Leahy Constitutional and Human Rights Law Collection, the S. Houston Lay Memorial International Law Library, and the Chin Kim Comparative Law Collection. Other naming gifts resulted in the Roy Morrow Bell Reading Room and the David and Constance Lam Clapp Board Room, as well as the Swortwood Bookstore and the Thomas E. Miller Mock Trial Room.

By the end of 1994, the Campaign for Excellence, with the major stalwart efforts of Mary Rand Williams, Executive Director of Development and Alumni Relations, and Communications Director Martha Ehringer, reached its two million dollar goal. Along with the now regular and material annual contributions, the successful conclusion of that Campaign crowned Dessent's efforts to achieve substantial giving to the school by its alumni and friends, which had never before been accomplished. In the decade preceding Dessent's tenure, total funds raised had been $50,000, while during his term of office over $4,000,000 had been raised!

Leaving no stone unturned as a fundraiser, Dessent had also helped form a committee to receive contributions to the law school from my students, friends and family. In a formal ceremony, the erstwhile Masonic Ceremonial Room and one-time School for Performing Arts theater was dedicated as the Professor George N. Gafford Moot Court Room. The Dean and Judge David Zenoff, along with two former students, Bob Fredrick, '73 and Rob Kilborne, '79, expressed warm sentimental phrases and reminiscences. Crowding out my thoughts of gratitude were the memories of all the problems and struggles we had endured to convert that neo-Italian Renaissance room into a court room and to preserve it and the integrity of the very school itself through all its jeopardous vicissitudes—and the hundreds of students and judges involved in all the trials conducted in that room.

With the substantially increased enrollment resulting from both Dessent's efforts and the increase nationally in law school applications, and the never-before major unearned augmentation of the budget from fundraising, the school's operating budget had in Dessent's tenure increased from $4,400,000 to $15,700,000!

During the period that Dessent was dean, faculty salaries had increased from being close to the bottom to the top one third in California, the faculty had grown from twenty-two to forty-six members, and the number of faculty women from 23% to 49%. At the same time the percentage of minority students had gone from 5% to 27%, and the mean GPA and LSAT scores of entering students had likewise increased dramatically.

It had obviously been the path to statistics like these that had impelled the faculty to recommend unanimously that he be reappointed as dean when as Board chairman I had asked for their feelings at the end of his first contract. At that time they had already credited him with a remarkable list of accomplishments in faculty leadership and rapport, in recruitment and public relations, in creating an endowment and development program, and in leading the school from a deficit to a substantial surplus.

But the strange dynamics of the relationship between a law faculty and its dean were a wonder to behold. The bonuses offered and paid for specific faculty efforts such as publishing books, writing articles and conducting conferences, at first happily responded to and received, became contentious as to comparative quality and worth. Even the formerly much-appreciated compliments and support of the faculty were labeled as insincere. Once the faculty salaries had been brought to appropriate competitive levels and were not continuously increased in large increments, the major previous increases were almost forgotten. The well-known syndrome "What have you done for me lately ?" slowly began to set in.

At the same time, undoubtedly, the equally well-known lessening with time of the enthusiasm and new ideas of any executive was slowly overtaking the dean. It was reported that his enormous early ebullience was waning, that his formerly incredibly long hours of work were shortening, and that his early strong rapport with the faculty was diminishing. There were even growing complaints of favoritism, of lack of respect for the faculty as a whole.

So it was that by the end of his eighth year as dean (which was already more than two and a half times the length of the average U. S. law school dean's tenure) murmurs of dissatisfaction reached the ears of the Board. It is questionable whether Dessent would have wanted any more, but at any rate his third contract was for only two years, resulting in a long and successful ten-year tenure, after which he seemed desirous and more than satisfied to join the faculty as a full professor.

Put in perspective, those ten years provided other most significant changes which took the law school to its next plateau and brought it effectively into its own as the sound institution vainly hoped for and envisioned when we purchased it, so close to death in 1975, from USIU.

None were left in the administration and to those few of us left on the faculty or the Board who well remembered when the faculty went unpaid, when the students withheld their tuition, when library creditors stopped deliveries and students had to tear up floors and strip paint, any current problems or complaints seemed minor indeed!

In its second decade as an independent law school, California Western's student body had increased from less than five hundred to eight hundred, cash and securities from $259,000 to $9,700,000, and most importantly, the total fund balances from $3,193,000 to $33,700,000! The stately old building which had once been a Masonic Temple had been substantially restored and made more functional, and together with the handsome new Campus Center made California Western School of Law a prominent downtown landmark.

All these changes and growth of the school over the years were somewhat paralleled in its commencement exercises. While it was still a part of USIU, the law school's graduates received their diplomas along with all of USIU's other graduates. The ceremonies were held in the Greek Theater of old Theosophical Society days on the Point Loma campus. Only the names of Cal Western's graduates, without any information about them, were listed along with the hundreds of other USIU graduates. While it was always very beautiful because of the setting among the trees on a cliff overlooking the ocean, it was usually a very long and rather tiresome proceeding.

After the purchase of the law school and its operation as an independent institution, the graduation exercises were held in the magnificent outdoor Organ Pavilion of Balboa Park, with its beautiful Spanish buildings and its pools and gardens in downtown San Diego. Following the ceremonies, there were receptions for the graduates and their families back at the law school. As the school grew and prospered, the event became more elaborate and with greater meaning for the students.

Designed by the same student who had designed the school's stained glass window in Diane's memory, a colorful banner on a staff is now carried at the head of the academic procession, the faculty wears purple robes, and for some years the receptions were held at the impressive outdoor sculpture garden of the San Diego Museum of Art, a few steps from the Organ Pavilion. For a few years the exercises were moved indoors to the Hotel del Coronado, where the proceedings and reception also made the proceedings enjoyable and memorable for the graduates and their loved ones.

Just as everything about the school had become more established, more dignified and more professional, so it was at commencement—here too the school had come of age. The proceedings were more formal and the receptions in excellent taste. Greater attention was paid to the Commencement programs, which now contained photographs and personal information about each graduate, and more interesting and celebrated individuals were the speakers and recipients of honorary degrees. Among the latter were such people as the Chief Justice and Justices of California's Supreme Court, United

States Court of Appeals Judges, an Attorney General of the United States, governors and other federal and state officials.

The traditional Sir Edward Elgar's *Pomp and Circumstance*, played on the mighty organ in Balboa Park, has been the processional music of choice for more than half the commencement exercises of the last thirty years, interspersed with such music as Clarke's *Prince of Denmark March* and Handel's *March From Occasional Suite* and his suite from *Water Music*. Not being included in the same ceremony among hundreds or thousands of graduates of other schools, the graduates of California Western School of Law receive their degrees in exercises completely their own and they alone are the center of attention, as on that day they should be.

But with the departure of Mike Dessent as dean, the faculty seemed to have the idea that what the school now needed was someone who from their perspective would be more of an "academic." They went to great lengths in preparing a profile of the sort of dean they sought, a profile and job description that could have been filled by only a very few of history's greatest world leaders!

With financial and organizational stability achieved, the stage was set for a different kind of dean.

For the first time, and with considerable trepidation, the Board of Trustees decided to engage the services of an agency, so-called "head hunters," to find a new dean. The Board determined that the additional expense was necessary because, as was not unusual, several law schools were at that time also seeking new deans, and independent California Western required more than the typical dean serving under a university umbrella.

The Board had hoped that professional "head hunters" would find desirable candidates outside the normal channels, candidates with different backgrounds as well as deans or professors of other schools, particularly since the managing of California Western required additional less-conventional abilities and experience.

But that hope had been in vain, for despite very elaborate brochures, curricula vitae, candidate profiles and conferences, suggestions and advice, the faculty was ultimately presented with three very eligible candidates from academia, probably no different than would have been obtained through the normal channels of a search committee's advertising and word of mouth.

Chapter XV

Another Dean and New Horizons as the Millennium Ends

As the result of the dean search conducted by the head-hunting firm, the California Western faculty recommended three former law school deans. From among those three, the Board of Trustees chose Steven R. Smith to succeed Mike Dessent. Smith had been dean of the Cleveland-Marshall Law School of Cleveland State University (where I had taught part-time for so many years when it was still an independent night law school). He had previously been a law professor at the University of Louisville, where he'd also served as Associate Dean and Acting Dean.

Smith had earned his B.A. at Buena Vista College, and his M.A. and J.D. at the University of Iowa. He developed the acclaimed Medical Institute for law faculty with the Cleveland Clinic Foundation, and had published widely in law and psychology and law and medicine.

An experienced administrator and teacher, Smith had been very active with the American Bar Association and the Association of American Law Schools, having served for one year with the latter as Deputy Director. Although he'd never been in business or practiced law, he nevertheless added a new dimension to the school, with different talents and some different priorities from Dean Dessent's.

In a flurry of mixed metaphors, it seemed to me that just as Dean Swortwood had given a premature infant reborn after a long sleep to Dean Castetter, he had handed a fully-weaned but rebellious young adolescent to Dean Friesen. Friesen in turn had passed on to Dean

Dessent an ambitious work-in-progress, and Dessent had provided Dean Smith with a well-equipped and fully-trained combat squadron, now ready to do battle!

It had been hoped, and it soon became evident, that Steve's close association with the ABA and the AALS would be of great value. Although the school's earlier problems with those institutions were long gone, their criticism of the library facilities was continuing. Also, their approval of any library plans, of the continuing MCL/LLM degree program for international lawyers, as well as of future Master of Laws graduate programs, would be greatly facilitated by the knowledge and relationships of the new dean.

His early focus was on formulating the mission of the law school, and he worked diligently with the faculty to create a feasible set of principles which would identify the objectives of the faculty for its students and at the same time set the school apart from others. Committees and retreats, meetings and preliminary drafts ultimately resulted in a very comprehensive document which can be distilled to one phrase: educate students to become lawyers who are creative problem solvers. It was some time before that mission was refined and developed to become something meaningful rather than esoteric, and a viable program fabricated.

Ultimately the McGill Center for Creative Problem Solving (named after William McGill, UCSD's third Chancellor and later President of Columbia University) was established and a grant of $750,000 received from the Weingart Foundation to support its work.

During Steve Smith's first year two new summer programs were added to introduce applicants to the school and prepare them for the strains of law school. The Transition and the Enrichment Programs, both of which made a significant difference in the entering class, were highly praised and had a positive impact on admissions.

The Master of Comparative Law and Master of Laws degree programs for international lawyers were submitted to the ABA and AALS and ultimately approved by them in 1998. During its first ten years, from 1984 to 1994, before its formal approval, a total of fifty-six foreign students participated, after which it was quiescent for almost four years. After the acquiescence by the ABA and AALS to the program, Professor Jackie Slotkin was put in charge, and it came into its own. By the spring of 2000, thirty-two students were in attendance, from Pakistan, Thailand, Lebanon, Switzerland, France, India, Germany, Mexico, Denmark, England, Japan, and Korea.

Discussions were continued with UCSD regarding cooperation and exchange of faculty, and a new agreement for the Juris Doctorate/Masters in Social Work dual degree program was entered into with San Diego State University.

In a new direction, California Western joined in the establishment of the first major consortium (that word again!) among one university-affiliated and four independent law schools named the Consortium for Innovative Legal Education. The other four schools are William Mitchell College of Law in St. Paul, Minnesota, South Texas College of Law in Houston, Texas, New England School of Law in Boston, Massachusetts and Stetson University College of Law in St. Petersburg, Florida.

California Western's success and satisfaction under Mike Dessent with the international faculty exchange program with Victoria University in Wellington, New Zealand, encouraged the planned interchange of students and faculty among the schools of the consortium. In addition, joint international programs (summer and semester abroad) are being undertaken, as well as Master of Laws modules and programs to improve faculty interaction. Also being explored are other mutually beneficial and uncharted areas of cooperation.

Of major importance to the future of the school, the dean and faculty presented to the Board of Trustees their recommendations for a new building on the property owned by the law school on the third corner of the intersection of Cedar Street and Third Avenue. The plans were for a four-storey structure devoted exclusively to a new law library. Also presented were recommendations for new classrooms and office uses for the vacated library space and further remodeling of the original 350 Cedar Street building. With the approval of the Board, faculty committees went forward with cost computations, recommendations of architects, and further studies.

It was determined that the school would establish a new program to permit students to attend Cal Western part-time, not as a traditional night school, but during the day, and formal application was made to the ABA and AALS for their approval.

There was continued improvement in the recruiting of minority students, with 33% and then 36% in the entering classes, and significant improvements were made in the career planning services of the school with the appointment of a new director and a doubling of the number of campus interviews by prospective employers.

Coincident with the new dean's tenure but in no way connected to it there was arising among the law school's students a new direction which I found disturbing. My concern was that it may represent a tendency toward segregation and Balkanization of the student body and away from the inclusiveness for which so many had fought for so many years. Or was it a new phenomenon that does not promote exclusivity but some sort of helpful rather than harmful joining of like-minded people in good faith?

Among "Student Organizations" in a recent school bulletin are found the following, listed alphabetically: Bisexual, Gay and Lesbian Student Association, Black Law Students Association, Hawai'i Law Students Association, Jewish Student Union, La Raza Student Association, Latter-day Saint Student Association, Pan Asian Student Bar Association, Persian Law Students Association, South Asian Law Students Association, and Women's Law Caucus!

Also listed are organizations with the far more obvious purpose of providing for students with common interests: American Trial Lawyers Association, Amnesty International, Association for Public Interest Law, Center for Telecommunications Law, Commentary, Criminal Justice Society, Entertainment and Sports Law Society, Environmental Law Society, Family Law Society, International Law Society, Intellectual Property Law Association, Lambda Alpha International Student Association, Law Review/International Law Journal, Legal

Skills Honors Instructors, Parents in Law School, Phi Alpha Delta, Phi Delta Phi, Student Ambassador Program, Student Bar Association, Student Tutors, and Surfing and Ocean Advocacy. These appear to me to be laudable and salutary.

But the proliferation of the organizations with what the Supreme Court has called "suspect" classifications when governmentally imposed disturbs me. These many religious, sexual/gender, and ethnic separations seem to be making a patchwork quilt of the great American melting pot we've so far struggled successfully to achieve. What is more they would appear to support those who have accepted discrimination and opposed desegregation by saying "They really want to be *with their own kind.*"

It seems to me that the objective of lawyers in a society such as ours should be to reduce and minimize our differences, homogenize our society rather than fractionalize it. The teachings of most of our schools have in recent years been in the direction of desegregation on the basis of race, religion, ethnic origin and sexual preference—and for the most part they are being successful if they are not derailed.

Every group identifiable on the basis of race, religion, ethnic origin and sexual preference in the United States has for years sought to prevent discrimination and to become an integrated part of the whole. The drive has been to abolish discrimination and different treatment of the various minorities and identifiable groups in order to prevent friction and achieve true equality of opportunity. The very formation and promotion of groups by themselves on their own initiative which would appear to classify and emphasize their "suspect" classifications so bravely sought to be erased seems most inappropriate for students of the United States Constitution and prospective lawyers.

It appears to me that since the findings of illegality of discrimination based on these classifications have been achieved under both state and federal law, there is no longer any need for the formation or maintenance of such groups for that purpose. And if they now have the purpose of seeking special advantages for them over other groups or over the majority, such reverse discrimination ought not be countenanced or fostered by law students.

Among the many achievements under Dean Smith's tenure for which he should be credited were increased participation by the faculty in national legal education. Barbara Cox served on the AALS Membership Review (Accreditation) Committee, Jan Stiglitz on the ABA Bar Admissions Committee, John Noyes on the AALS Scholarly Paper Committee, Phyllis Marion (the new Library Director) on the AALS 2000 Annual Meeting Planning Committee, and Linda Morton chaired the ABA Externship Committee. Steve himself served on the ABA Council of the Section of Legal Education and Admissions to the Bar.

Carrying on Dessent's efforts to increase the visibility of the law school within the legal profession, a new magazine, Res Ipsa, was launched. It was intended to promote the school nationally as well as locally, being mailed to alumni, judges and national bar leaders.

But Smith's primary emphasis both to better the school's program for its students and improve its reputation was on the school's stated mission, training lawyers to become creative problem solvers. After the school's receipt of the substantial foundation grant, Jamie Cooper joined the McGill Center for Creative Problem Solving as Executive Director, with Professors Janeen Kerper serving as Academic Director and Janet Bowermaster as Research Director.

Cooper came to the law school with great experience and excellent credentials. Both a barrister and solicitor with undergraduate and graduate degrees from the University of Toronto and the University of Cambridge, he first worked for Baker and McKenzie, our nation's largest law firm. He had lectured on law, lawyering and foreign affairs at the University of Strathclyde in Glasgow and King's College, University of London among others in the United Kingdom. He had also lectured to such organizations as the Conference on Contemporary Canadian Affairs, American Psychology and Law Association and Hofstra University in North America, and the Faculty of Law of the Catholic University of Milan and the Department of Legal Philosophy at the University of Florence in Italy.

He had been a delegate to the World Congress on Social Philosophy and the Law at the University of Iceland and to the United Nations Congress on Public International Law. More recently Cooper has presented papers at the *Global Meeting of Generations* conference for the United Nations Development Program, the *Future of War* conference in St. Petersburg, Russia, and the *Hague Appeal for Peace*.

Soon the grand and noble plan of the McGill Center began to take shape. Creative Problem Solving was given a broad definition:

"An intellectual discipline that requires lawyers to define problems so as to permit the broadest possible array of solutions, both legal and nonlegal. Creative Problem Solving seeks many points of view, and systematically examines problems for their relational implications at the individual, institutional and societal levels. It seeks caring solutions that are novel or transformative in nature.

"Creative Problem Solving is an evolving global approach to resolving conflict in society. Creative Problem Solving approaches problems holistically so as to resolve all aspects of a given conflict, drawing on all disciplines to heal society and fuse together the ever-changing world around us."

Certainly no one could quarrel with such lofty aims and every effort was to be expended to implement their fruition. Focus groups were formed locally, nationally and internationally, and gradually the role of lawyers and of law schools was evolved. Law schools were to foster creativity in divesting preconceptions, look to novel approaches to problems, consider alternatives to the traditional case method approach by teaching preventive law, interactive client relations, and alternative dispute resolution.

With Latin American judges and lawyers the McGill Center has partnered with the Universidad Catolica de Temuco, Chile, to create *Proyecto Acceso*. Seeking to establish a Latin American center for the training of jurists as more open adversarial-based systems are replacing traditional Latin American inquisitorial systems, *Proyecto Acceso* will focus on advocacy, problem solving, mediation and arbitration.

Together with Mexico a Binational Mediation Team has been created to facilitate dialogue across the border, stem unnecessary cross-border litigation, foster U.S./Mexican judicial exchange conferences and promote continued growth and collaboration in the frontier areas.

Under Jamie Cooper's direction the Center sponsors a variety of programs ranging from working with the public schools and local and national institutions to looking at international terrorism. With the Center's Youth Voices video series, a high school curriculum on Creative Problem Solving is being developed to provide young people with the tools for successful and constructive non-violent lives. The Center's substantial grant has also enabled it to work with the law school faculty toward defining and conceptualizing creative problem solving, and it has promoted publication in the California Western Law Review of a symposium focused on the lawyer as problem solver.

With Professor Bowermaster as the Center's Research Director, a study has been made of the impact of domestic violence on children and its consideration as a factor in custody determinations by the courts. Another research project has been a study of the effects of mediation in the San Diego Superior Court to seek to determine whether certain mediations settle more frequently than others, and why.

Historically the appellate cases read by law students have been used as the vehicle by which they learn the precedents of the common law and the methods of its reasoning. However, it has long been my thought, and certainly the thought of many others, that as successful as that method has been, it has its shortcomings. These have been attempted to be cured by individual law teachers with the use of a variety of other teaching devices.

As I have said before, learning the law from the reading of appellate cases with the strong accent on who won and who lost and why, leads to an emphasis on litigation. Too often the students have been taught only to use the learning from those cases for the purpose of winning or successfully defending such lawsuits, rather than how to avoid them altogether. If Jamie Cooper is able successfully to encourage law teachers to emphasize and impart to their students the changed emphasis in the cases by calling it creative problem solving, nothing could please me more. That is what I have consistently sought to do and advocated to *avoid* litigation, for that is what I believe to be the most common reason lawyers ought to be retained and the greatest service they can provide.

Also, with greater knowledge of the case law can come the greater ability to solve controversies that could not be avoided by methods other than litigation, such as mediation and arbitration, which are now being taught in most law schools as Alternative Dispute Resolution. It would also be my wish that the necessity and the art of *compromise* could also somehow be taught—to both lawyers and their clients!

At any rate, to the extent that the Center for Creative Problem Solving will actually lead to better solutions to the many problems of living in an organized society with its penchant for disagreement and dispute, it cannot but be applauded.

As an outgrowth of the original Emil Brown Mock Law Office competition, soon named the Client Counseling Competition, in which two Cal Western teams won national victories in its early years, has come the National Center for Preventive Law. As a result of Jamie Cooper's and Tom Barton's working with the Louis Brown family, California Western has now become the home of the National Center, with its emphasis on client counseling and preventive law.

Perhaps the day will come when being a party to a lawsuit will be looked upon as having failed, which is already the view in some societies. It is to be hoped that the Center for Creative Problem Solving and the National Center for Preventive Law will together provide the stimulus for California Western to lead in the study and the teaching of the prevention of litigation and the solution of controversy.

But until that time arrives, and even when it does, there will be controversies which are impossible of avoidance or solution, primarily where the facts are in dispute, where amounts or principles are impossible of accommodation, or new legal interpretations sought. These must ultimately be tried in one of the greatest of institutions, our courts of law. Whether before a judge or a jury, the litigants require counsel, and it is then the obligation of lawyers competently to represent their clients to the best of their ability—and there law schools must lead in their early trial training.

From the law school's earliest boards, the few diligent stalwarts persuaded to serve the newly-independent law school without any financial contribution, meeting in the then ill-furnished Reading Room, to the most participatory and generous board at the end of the century, sitting at the handsome horseshoe table in the contemporary board room, is as great a study in contrasts as everything else about the school. As the result of the incredible efforts of Trustees Connie Clapp and Roy Black and Development Director Kerri Van Duyne, the unanimous board contributed more than three-quarters of a million dollars to the law school's Campaign Twenty One![35] And a year later an anonymous donor gave one and a quarter million dollars in honor of Dean and Marj Castetter.

The most visible and permanent additions to the law school during Steve Smith's tenure are the completion of the remodeling and refurbishing of the 350 Cedar building and the addition of the third building to the now impressive campus of California Western School

---

[35] On that century-ending board of twenty-six members were University of Denver Professor Bill Beaney, San Diego attorney and former Board chairman Roy Bell, Las Vegas attorney Neil Beller, retired busines executive and Chairman Emeritus Roy Black, Honolulu business man Han Ching, New York retired investment banker Connie Clapp, the author, retired banker and former Board chairman Murray Galinson, U.S. District Judge Irma Gonzalez, Oceanside attorney and present Board chairman Ken Greenman, UCSD architect Boone Hellman, Santa Barbara attorney Jim Herman, U.S. District Judge Napoleon Jones, Las Vegas attorney Randall Jones, prominent San Diego attorney Jeff Lewin, U. S. District Judge Jim Lorenz, former Congressman Jim Lowery, recent student San Diego attorney Jerrilyn Malana, San Diego attorney and developer Mark Mandell, Houston attorney Jeff Newport, Newport Beach attorney Bob Scott, retired business executive Gene Step, U.S. Magistrate Jim Stiven, CPA Jim West, retired Judge Howard Weiner, and Deputy Court Administrator Arnold Winston.

of Law—hardly even imaginable to those who have known and seen it from its early beginnings through its arduous and nearly-futile struggles!

The entry lobby of the 350 Cedar building has been beautifully renovated, many rooms remodeled and upgraded, with the exterior of the building substantially repaired and repainted. Along with upgrading of the air conditioning and other mechanical services, the space vacated by the library was reconfigured. One large new classroom was built, plus a smaller classroom, two seminar rooms, student organization space, adjunct faculty offices and new quarters for the McGill Center.

The new library building was completed in December of 1999, and the library moved into it from the 350 Cedar building. After its official opening at the very inception of the new millennium, it was later dedicated by Supreme Court Justice Anthony M. Kennedy in an impressive formal ceremony. The attractive building is the most efficient and useful that could be designed for the present and future, with every provision for both electronic and hard-cover research. Aesthetically and ergonomically admirable and distinctive, it is a four-storey building which with the other two will ultimately blend in style and color on the three corners of the cohesive intersection.

These three buildings now form the handsome downtown San Diego campus of the tiny proprietary night school whose growth and shifting sands have been chronicled from its uncertain beginnings and almost insurmountable travails, to its unprecedented purchase from a university and its maturing into a unique independent law school. Through these incredible perils of Pauline and tempered on the anvils of adversity, it has ultimately became financially sound and fully staffed, with a scholarly and mission-oriented faculty in its teaching and its publishing, contributing to the community and the profession and offering excellent legal education in handsome and efficient facilities. All its students, alumni and faculty, and all who have been connected with it have a right to be proud.

About the Author

The author is a graduate of Yale College and Case Western Reserve University law school, was an attorney with the U.S. Securities and Exchange Commission and a civilian investigator with the Army Air Corps, and served in the U.S. Navy during World War II as a deck officer and as a military governor in Korea immediately thereafter.

He was in the private practice of the law for close to twenty five years, Assistant Attorney General of Ohio, and adjunct professor at Cleveland College, Ohio College of Podiatry, Case Western Reserve law school, and Cleveland Marshall (now Cleveland Sate) law school. After eighteen years as a full-time law professor at California Western School of Law, he has served as Chairman and has been a member of the school's Board of Trustees since 1987.